PUFFIN BOOKS
GREAT PUFFIN JOKE DIRECTORY

This is the funniest reference book you've ever read. There are hundreds of jokes of every kind in the Great Joke Directory, the world's funniest A–Z of jokes. And there are even a few X-rated jokes *not* to be told to grannies, mums and dads, or grown-ups of any kind – or teachers!

From aeroplanes to zebras, from anacondas to zzubs, there's a joke to tell!

BROUGH GIRLING was born in 1946, and now lives in London with his wife and a mad cat. As well as writing books he has been head of the Children's Book Foundation, and was the first editor of Young Telegraph. He is founder and director of Readathon, the national sponsored read that raises money for charity.

GREAT PUFFIN JOKE DIRECTORY

Brough Girling

Illustrated by Alan Rowe

Puffin Books

PUFFIN BOOKS

Published by the Penguin Group
Penguin Books Ltd, 27 Wrights Lane, London W8 5TZ, England
Penguin Books USA Inc., 375 Hudson Street, New York, New York 10014, USA
Penguin Books Australia Ltd, Ringwood, Victoria, Australia
Penguin Books Canada Ltd, 10 Alcorn Avenue, Toronto, Ontario, Canada M4V 3B2
Penguin Books (NZ) Ltd, 182–190 Wairau Road, Auckland 10, New Zealand

Penguin Books Ltd, Registered Offices: Harmondsworth, Middlesex, England

First published 1990
10 9 8 7 6 5

Text copyright © Brough Girling, 1990
Illustrations copyright © Alan Rowe, 1990
All rights reserved

Printed in England by Clays Ltd, St Ives plc
Filmset in Monophoto Plantin

For
Miss Louisa Shaw

INTRODUCTION

Welcome to the *world's funniest reference book*!

Using this GREAT JOKE DIRECTORY you can find out what's gigglesome about anything from Aardvarks to bees flying backwards – Zzub zzub!

Look out too for brand new jokes, classroom fresh, and our amazing Fascinating Facts!

Find out what Humpty did with his hat!

Discover the name of the world's only one-eyed dinosaur!

ONE THOUSAND JOKES AND NOT ALL ABOUT ELEPHANTS!

In compiling this book I am especially grateful to my friend Major Obstacle. The Major is President of the Society for the Preservation of Old Jokes and is a leading authority on what waiters say when men in restaurants complain about flies in their soup (see page 64). He is also famous for his Save the Chicken Crossing the Road for the Nation Campaign.

Being an authority on medieval and prehistoric jokes – often known as 'Old Chestnuts' – Major Obstacle has awarded special Old Chestnut Awards to his favourite hard-wearing jokes. Beware: your mum and dad may have heard some of them before.

A

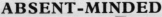

NO GREAT JOKE DIRECTORY COULD START WITHOUT AN AARDVARK JOKE!

AARDVARK
Knock knock!
Who's there?
Aardvark.
Aardvark who?
Aardvark a million miles for one of your smiles!

ABSENT-MINDED
An **absent-minded** professor went to have
supper with a friend. There was a terrible
snowstorm that evening, and towards midnight
the professor's host suggested that he should stay
the night because of the bad weather.

'*Thank you*,' said the professor. '*I'll just go
home and get my toothbrush and pyjamas.*'

ACCIDENTS
A cowboy was being examined by his doctor.

'Yours is a very dangerous life,' said the
doctor. 'Have you had many **accidents**?'

'Nope!' said the cowboy.

'Has nothing horrible ever happened to you?'

'Well, I was once kicked by my horse, and
another time a rattlesnake bit me.'

'Don't you call those accidents?' said the

doctor in amazement.

'Nope,' said the cowboy. '*They did it on purpose!*'

A man was in court for having caused a road
accident. 'When you arrived at the roundabout,
what gear were you in?' asked the judge.

'*Well*,' replied the man. '*I think it was green
trousers, a white shirt and these shoes.*'

ADAM
What did **Adam** say on the day before
Christmas?
'*It's Christmas Eve!*'

ADULTS
Why are **adults** always complaining?
Because they are *groan ups*!

AEROPLANE
Who invented the first **aeroplane** that
couldn't fly?
The Wrong Brothers!

Two men were sitting in an **aeroplane**. 'Look,'
said one of them who was sitting by a window.
'Those people down there are so tiny – they look
like ants.'

'They *are* ants, you fool,' said the other man,
'*we haven't taken off yet!*'

ALLIGATOR
What did the elephant say to the **alligator** when
it bit his trunk off?
'*I subbose you fink dat's funny!*'

THAT REMINDS ME OF A KNOCK KNOCK JOKE:

Knock knock!
Who's there?
Althea.
Althea who?
*Althea later, **alligator**!*

▷ **see Crocodile jokes on page 41**

ALPHABET

MAN IN RESTAURANT: Waiter, there's a bee in my soup.
WAITER: *Yes, sir, it's **alphabet** soup!*

FATHER: 'Why are you taking so long with that **alphabet** soup, son?'
SON: *'I'm eating it alphabetically.'*

AMBIDEXTROUS

I'D GIVE MY RIGHT HAND TO BE AMBIDEXTROUS!

AMEN

Why do we say **'amen'** not 'awomen'?
Because we sing hymns not hers!

AMERICA

FASCINATING FACT: The two biggest women in **America** are Miss Oury and Mrs Sippy!

What's big and black and hairy and flies to
America?
King Kongcorde!

ANACONDA

What do you get if you cross an **anaconda** with
a glow worm?
A thirty-foot strip light!

ANCESTORS

I CAN TRACE MY ANCESTORS BACK TO ROYALTY.

CAN YOU? KING KONG?!

ANDES

TEACHER: Who can tell me where the **Andes** are?
BOY: *I can – they're on the end of your armies!*

ANIMALS

What **animals** like to play cricket?
Bats!

What big grey **animal** sits in rivers and
complains that it's ill?
A hippo-chondriac!

ANTI-FREEZE
TEACHER: How do you make **anti-freeze?**
BOY: *Lock her in the fridge!*

ANTS
What **ant** eats fish?
A cormorant!

What is an American **ant**?
The wife of an American uncle!

I SUPPOSE SOLDIER ANTS ARE CALLED COMBAT-ANTS?

WHAT AN IGNORANT BIRD YOU ARE!

ANTS – DEAD
Who sings about **dead ants**?
*The Pink Panther: Dead-ant, dead-ant, deadant
deadant deadant dead-ant dead-ant deadant
deadant.*

APES
A small boy went into the kitchen and asked his
mother: 'Mummy, my teacher says we are
descended from the **apes**. Is that true?'
    'I don't know, dear,' replied his mother, '*I
never met your father's family!*'

APPENDICITIS

DOCTOR: Miss Jones, you have acute **appendicitis**.

MISS JONES: *Never mind the compliments, what's wrong with me?*

APPLE

Doctor, doctor, I think I'm an **apple**.
Well sit down, I won't bite you!

I KNOW HOW TO MAKE AN APPLE PUFF. CHASE IT ROUND THE KITCHEN.

FASCINATING FACT: An **apple** a day keeps the doctor away, an onion a day keeps *everyone* away!

Apples put colour into your cheeks.

BUT I DON'T WANT GREEN CHEEKS!

ARCHAEOLOGIST

Doctor, doctor, I'm an **archaeologist**.
So what?
My career is in ruins!

THAT JOKE'S INFRADIG!

ARITHMETIC

What tool do you need for **arithmetic**?
Multi-pliers!

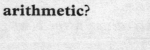

ARROWS

A motorist turned the wrong way into a one-way street. 'Didn't you see the **arrows**?' demanded a policeman crossly.

'*Arrows?*' said the motorist. '*I didn't even see any Indians!*'

▭▷ **this way to another One-Way Street joke on page 124**

ASPIRIN

Why should you never leave a box of **aspirins** near a bird cage?
The parrots-eat-'em-all!

> OH, I GET IT - PARACETAMOL!

Why did the skunk take an **aspirin**?
He had a stinking headache.

ASTRONAUT

How do you get a baby **astronaut** to go to sleep?
Rocket!

AUTHORS

> HAVE YOU READ ANY OF THE FOLLOWING BOOKS WRITTEN BY FAMOUS AUTHORS? IF NOT, GO DOWN AND ASK FOR THEM AT YOUR LOCAL LIBRARY. THE LIBRARIAN WILL BE SO PLEASED!

Falling Off a Cliff by Eileen Dover

Get Rich Quick by Robin Banks

Expedition to the North Pole by Ann Tartic

How to Feed Dogs by Nora Bone

The Tiger's Revenge by Claude Leg

Be Prepared by Justin Case

Crime Prevention by Ivor Truncheon and
Laura Norder

Improve Your Memory by L. E. Phant

Keeping Pet Snakes by Sir Pent

Party Games by Hans Knees and Bumpsa Daisy

Great Murder Mysteries by Ivor Clue

More Great Murder Mysteries by Hugh Dunnit

Growing Vegetables by Rosa Cabbages

Daft Jokes by M. T. Head

Steel Bands by Lydia Dustbin

Ghost Stories by I. M. Scared

Chinese Window Cleaning by Who Flung Dung

Shipwrecks by Mandy Lifeboats

How to be a Waiter by Roland Butter

Famous Pirates by R. Jimlad

B

BABY
What were the policeman's **baby's** first three words?
Hallo! Hallo! Hallo!

BAGPIPES

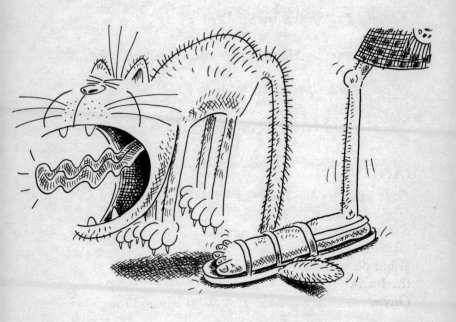

> **FASCINATING FACT: Bagpipes** were
> invented by an ancient Scotsman who stood
> on an ancient Scottish cat's tail.

BANANA

HAVE YOU HEARD ABOUT THE MAN WHO WENT TO THE DOCTOR AND TOLD HIM THAT HE THOUGHT HE WAS TURNING INTO A BANANA?

NO.

THE DOCTOR TOLD HIM TO SLIP BEHIND THE SCREEN AND PEEL HIS CLOTHES OFF!

If you can make shoes from crocodile skins, what can you make from **banana** skins?
Slippers!

BANANA SPLIT

What's a **banana split** called when you drop it from the top of a skyscraper on to the pavement below?
A banana splat!

BANDSTAND

How do you make a **bandstand**?
Hide all their chairs!

BANK

What do you call a man with a large overdraft at the **bank**?
Owen!

BARBER'S SHOP

A small cheeky boy went into a **barber's shop** and sat in a chair. 'Would you like a hair-cut, sonny?' said the barber.
'*I'd like them **all** cut please!*' said the boy.

Another small cheeky boy went into *another* **barber's shop** and sat in the chair. 'How would you like your hair cut?' asked the barber.

'*Off!*' said the boy.

BARGAIN
A **bargain** hunter always bought anything that was marked down. Last week she went into a department store and came out with an escalator!

BARREL
What can you put in a **barrel** that will make it lighter?
A hole.

BATH
Why did the robber take a **bath**?
So he could make a clean getaway!

BATHROOM
'Hey Dad, come quick, I've seen a horrible sight! Something is running across the **bathroom** floor – it's got no legs!'

'What are you talking about, son?'

'*Water!*'

BATSMEN
Why are **batsmen** cowards?
Because they are afraid of ducks!

BEACH
What did the sea say to the **beach**?
Nothing, *it just waved*.

BEANS

MAN IN RESTAURANT: Waiter, what's this?
WAITER: It's **bean** soup, sir.
MAN: *I don't care what it's been, what is it now?!*

BEARS

ADMIRING LADY: 'Have you ever hunted **bear**?'
HUNTER: *'No, I always wear a safari jacket and shorts.'*

FASCINATING FACT: If you cross a **bear** with a skunk, you get Winnie-the-Pooh.

The three **bears** came back from a teddy bears' picnic. 'Oh, no!' said Daddy Bear, 'Who's been eating my porridge?'

'And who's been eating MY porridge?' said Mummy Bear.

'Never mind the porridge,' said Baby Bear. *'Who's nicked the video?!'*

WINNIE-THE-POOH AND ALFRED THE GREAT HAVE ONE THING IN COMMON

WHAT?

THEIR MIDDLE NAME

BEAUTY PARLOUR

A woman walked into a **beauty parlour** and said to the girl behind the desk: 'Have you got anything that might improve my looks?'

'How about "distance"?' said the girl.

BEEF

ADVERT: BUY MORE BEEF: IT'S PERFECT FOR SUNDAY – THE DAY OF *ROAST*!

BEES

Why do **bees** hum?

They don't know the words!

What do you call a **bee** with a quiet hum?
A mumble bee!

BELL

What do you get if you cross a **bell** with a bee?
A hum-dinger!

BENGAL

There was a young man from **Bengal**
Who went to a fancy dress ball,
He thought he would risk it,
And go as a biscuit,
But the dog ate him up in the hall!

★ Old ★
Chestnut
Award

BICYCLE

FASCINATING FACT: A **bicycle** can't stand up on its own because it's too tired!

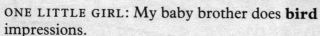

OH, I GET IT, 'TWO TYRED'!

BIRDS

What **birds** make lunches for people?
Cook-oos.

ONE LITTLE GIRL: My baby brother does **bird** impressions.
ANOTHER LITTLE GIRL: Really?
FIRST LITTLE GIRL: *Yes, he eats worms!*

Why do **birds** fly south in the winter?
It's too far to walk!

What **birds** fly around in formation, very fast?
The Red Sparrows!

I SUPPOSE WHEN THEY NEED TO BALE OUT THEY USE SPARROWCHUTES!

What **bird** terrified people in the Middle Ages?
Attila the Hen!

> **FASCINATING FACT:** If the sky wasn't so high, the **birds** would keep banging their heads.

BIRDS – PET

What do you get if you cross a **pet bird** with a fierce dog?
A budgerigrrrrrr!

BIRDSEED

A man walked into a pet shop. 'I'd like a box of **birdseed** please,' he said to the assistant.

'What sort of bird have you got, sir?' he asked.

'*None at the moment,*' said the man indignantly. '*I haven't even sown it yet.*'

BIRTHDAY

A man reached his hundredth **birthday**. 'If I'd known that I was going to live this long,' he told his friends, 'I'd have taken better care of myself!'

What do you get every **birthday**?
A year older.

BLACK AND WHITE

What's **black and white** and red all over?
A newspaper!

★ Old ★ Chestnut Award

What's **black and white** and red at the top?
A sunburnt puffin!

HEY, THAT'S NOT FUNNY!

What's **black and white** and red at the bottom?
A badger with nappy rash!

THAT IS!

What's **black and white** and black and white and black and white?
A nun rolling downhill!

BLOODHOUNDS

NEWSFLASH:
All the **bloodhounds** at Scotland Yard have been stolen. Police say they have no leads . . .

BLUE

OH, NO! A BLUE JOKE!

What's hairy, ugly and **blue**?
Roland Rat holding his breath!

BLUEBOTTLE

'I must fly,' said the **bluebottle**.
'O K,' said the bee. *'I'll give you a buzz later.'*

BOA CONSTRICTOR

Why did the two **boa constrictors** get married?
They had a crush on each other!

BOATING LAKE

'Come in number 9!' called out a man working at a **boating lake**.

'Hang on,' said his boss. 'We've only got seven boats!'

'Are you in trouble number 6?' shouted the man, looking worried.

BOOMERANG

How can you get rid of a **boomerang**?
Throw it down a one-way street!

What do you get if you cross a skunk with a **boomerang**?
A smell that is very difficult to get rid of!

 see more Skunk jokes on page 156

BOY GEORGE

Name two animals that **Boy George** sings about.
Camel camel camel camel camel camel lion!

24

BOY SCOUT

What do you get if you cross King Kong with a **boy scout**?

A kid in a uniform who throws old ladies across the road.

BRAKES

A policeman overtook a motorist in an old car, and stopped him.

'Why were you going so fast?' he asked sternly.

'Well, officer,' said the driver. *'This car hasn't got any* **brakes** *so I was hurrying home before I had an accident.'*

BREAKFAST

What is 600 feet high and pops up for **breakfast**?

The Toast Office Tower!

BRIDES

 BRIDES ARE VERY UNLUCKY, THEY NEVER MARRY THE BEST MAN!

BRIDGE

Doctor, doctor, I think I'm a **bridge**.

Now then, what's come over you?

So far, a bus and three cars.

BROSE

A boy came to school with a great big red swelling on the end of his nose. 'How did you get that?' asked a teacher.

'I was smelling a **brose**,' said the boy sadly.

'I think you mean ROSE,' replied the teacher. 'There's no "B" in rose.'

'*There was in this one!*' said the boy.

BROTHERS!

A lady was putting her coat on to go out. 'Where are you going, Mum?' asked her daughter.

'I'm taking your **brother** to the doctor's; I don't like the look of him.'

'*I'll come with you,*' replied the girl. '*I don't like the look of him either!*'

BUDGERIGAR

What should you do with a sick **budgerigar**?
Take it to a vet for tweetment!

BUILDING SITE

A teddy bear started working on a **building site**. During the morning he worked with the men digging a big trench for large pipes to go in. At lunch-time he put down his pickaxe and shovel and he and all the men went off to the pub.

When they came back the bear was horrified to see that his pickaxe was not where he had left it.

He went off to see the foreman, and explained the situation to him.

'Well, I'm not surprised,' said the foreman. 'Didn't you know – *today's the day the teddy bears have their picks nicked*!'

BULL

A woman was standing in a field when she noticed a **bull** at the other side of it.

'Is that bull safe?' she asked the farmer who was leaning on the gate.

'*Well,*' said the farmer. '*He's a lot safer than you are!*'

BULLDOZER

What do you call a man with a **bulldozer** on his head?
Squashed!

BUM

What comes from the desert and shouts '**bum**!'?
Very crude oil . . .

BURGLAR

JUDGE: Why did you take all this money?
BURGLAR: *I thought the change would do me good.*

What do you get if you cross a **burglar** with a bag of cement?
A hardened criminal.

BUS

A **bus** started out empty from the depot. At the first stop four men, three ladies and eight children got on. At the next stop six men, four ladies, three children and two dogs got on, and three children got off. At the third stop eight men, two ladies and no children or dogs got on, but three men and two ladies got off. At the next stop every single person, and the dogs, got off. Who was left on the bus?
All the married people!

> I GET IT, THE SINGLE PEOPLE HAD GOT OFF!

BUTCHER

A lady went into a **butcher's** shop and bought some steak. Then she asked the butcher if she could have some bits for her dog.

'Certainly, madam,' said the Butcher. *'Which bits is he missing?'*

ADVERT IN BUTCHER'S SHOP WINDOW:
PLEASED TO MEET YOU
MEAT TO PLEASE YOU!

A man went into a **butcher's** shop carrying a chicken he had bought the day before.

BUTTER

BUTTERFLY
What's pretty, with wings and a sub-machine gun?
A killer butterfly!

BUTTRESS
TEACHER: Sammy, what's a **buttress**?
SAMMY: *A female goat, Miss!*

C

CABBAGES

> HANG ON! THERE'S NOTHING FUNNY ABOUT CABBAGES.

> YES, THERE IS. WHAT DO YOU CALL TWO ROWS OF CABBAGES?

> I DON'T KNOW.

> A DUAL CABBAGEWAY!!

CAMEL

Why do **camels** wear sandals?
To stop themselves sinking into the sand.
Why do ostriches bury their heads in the sand?
To take a look at the **camels** *who forgot to put on their sandals!*

What do you call a **camel**
with three humps?
Humphrey!

Old *Chestnut Award*

FASCINATING FACT: If you cross a **camel** with a stupid cow you get thick, lumpy milkshakes.

How do you stop a **camel** passing through the eye of a needle?
Tie a knot in its tail!

CARDS
Doctor, doctor, I keep thinking I'm a pack of **cards**.
Sit down, I'll deal with you later.

CARS
Why is a baby like an old **car**?
They both have a rattle!

When do Japanese **car** parts fall out of the sky?
When it's raining Datsun Cogs!

Why can't **cars** play football?
They've only got one boot!

What do you call a man with a **car** on his head?
Jack!

CAST IRON SINKS

WE ALREADY KNOW THAT!

CATS

What is a **cat's** favourite TV programme?
Miami Mice!

And what do **cats** like for breakfast?
Mice Crispies, of course!!

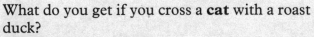

AND THEY READ THE MEWS OF THE WORLD!

What do you get if you cross a **cat** with a roast duck?
A duck-filled-fatty-puss!

THAT REMINDS ME

WHAT DO DUCKBILLED PLATYPUSSES HAVE THAT NO OTHER ANIMAL HAS?

BABY DUCKBILLED PLATYPUSSES!

When is it unlucky to see a black **cat**?
When you're a mouse!

I BOUGHT A CAT ONCE. BUT I TOOK IT BACK TO THE PET SHOP BECAUSE ALTHOUGH THE MAN THERE HAD TOLD ME THAT IT WOULD BE GOOD FOR MICE, IT NEVER SEEMED TO CATCH ANY. 'WELL', SAID THE MAN WHO SERVED ME. 'THAT'S GOOD FOR MICE ISN'T IT?!'

CHEATING

A teacher looked up from his desk while the children were doing an exam. 'James!' he said sternly. 'I hope I didn't just see you **cheating**.'

'*So do I!*' said James.

CHEESE

CHEMIST'S SHOP

A cat went into a
chemist's shop . . .

OH, YOU MEAN *PUSS IN BOOTS!!*

CHEWING GUM

SMALL BOY: My dad wanted to stop smoking,
so he tried **chewing gum**.
HIS FRIEND: Did it work?
SMALL BOY: No, *he couldn't get it to light*!

CHICKENS

'Bad news for **chickens**! Bad news for chickens!
– eggs are going up again!'

Why did the blind **chicken** cross the road?
To get to the bird's eye shop!

WHAT A FOWL JOKE.

▷ **see more Road jokes on page 145**

35

WHAT DO YOU EXPECT THEM TO DO, MOO?

CHIMNEY SWEEP

MAN: Do you like being a **chimney sweep**?
SWEEP: Yes, *it soots me!*

CHIP PAN

NEWSFLASH:
A mysterious object, shaped like a **chip pan**, was seen in the sky last night. The police say it may have been an Unidentified Frying Object.

CHIPS

A man sat down in a restaurant and ordered steak, **chips** and peas. The steak when it came was very small. When the man had finished a waiter came up and took his plate away. As he did so he asked: 'How did you find your steak, sir?'

'Easy,' said the man. '*I just moved a chip and there it was!*'

CINDERELLA

What song did **Cinderella** sing when she took her holiday films to the chemist's?

'*Some day my prints will come . . .*'

Why did **Cinderella** go to bed in the fireplace?
She wanted to sleep like a log!

CLEANER

HEAD TEACHER: Look at this classroom. It looks
as if it hasn't been cleaned for a fortnight!
SCHOOL CLEANER: Don't blame me, *I've only
been here a week!*

CLOWN

A **clown** took his car into a garage. 'What's the
matter with it?' asked the mechanic.

'Well,' said the clown, '*every time I kick it the
front wing doesn't fall off!*'

COAL

What kind of bird digs for **coal**?
A mynah bird!

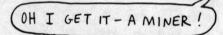
OH I GET IT – A MINER !

COAT OF ARMS

A **coat of arms** is what an octopus wears when
it's cold.

COD

> **FASCINATING FACT:** A mother **cod** lays two million eggs, and not one of her kids ever remembers Mother's Day.

A man was brought a very small piece of **cod** in a restaurant. It was cold, and grey and very unappetizing. He called the waiter over and said:
  'This piece of cod passeth all understanding!'

COFFEE

A man had finished his meal in a cafe. 'Waiter,' he said, 'bring me a **coffee**, without cream.'
  'I'm sorry, sir,' said the waiter. *'We've run out of cream, you'll have to have it without milk!'*

COFFIN

A hearse with a **coffin** in the back of it was going up a steep hill. Suddenly the back door came open and the coffin fell out and started slipping back down the road. The driver of the hearse leapt out and started chasing after it. 'Hey,' he yelled as he dashed past a chemist's shop, *'Have you got anything to stop this coffin?!'*

COOK

Knock knock!
Who's there?
Cook.
Cook who?
You're the first one I've heard this year!

SMALL GIRL: Our school **cook** is very cruel,
she beats the eggs and whips the cream.

COPPER NITRATE

CHEMISTRY TEACHER: What's **copper nitrate**?
BOY: *What policemen on night duty get paid!*

CORN FLAKES

WE'LL TELL YOU A REALLY GOOD JOKE ABOUT CORN FLAKES NEXT WEEK.

YES— IT'S A CEREAL!

COURT

Order! Order in **Court**!
  'I'll have fish and chips please, Guv,' said the
prisoner.

COWBOYS

ADVERT:
FAMOUS FILM:
THE COWBOY WITH NO MONEY
STARRING *SKINT EASTWOOD*

A **cowboy** was always claiming that he was the 'fastest gun in the West'. One day he came into a bar with his hands in plaster and his arm in a sling and a bandage round his head.

'What happened to you?' asked one of the men in the bar.

'I got beaten in a gun fight,' said the cowboy sadly.

'I thought you were the "fastest gun in the West"?'

'I am, *I was on holiday in the east when it happened*!'

What wears a **cowboy** hat, spurs and lives in the sea?
Billy the Squid!

FIRST **COWBOY**: You've put that saddle on backwards.
SECOND COWBOY: How do you know – *you don't even know which way I want to go*!

COWS

Why do **cows** have bells?
Their horns don't work!

FASCINATING FACT: **Cows** always lie down when it's raining. They do it to keep each udder dry.

What do you get if you cross a **cow** with a sheep and a goat?
The Milky Bar Kid!

Knock knock!
Who's there?
Cows.
Cows who?
No they don't, they moo!

What do you call a **cow** that eats your grass?
A lawn moo-er!

CRICKET

Why does the English **cricket** team need
cigarette lighters?
They've lost all their matches!

CROCODILES

What is a **crocodile's** favourite game?
Snap!

A woman went into a shoe shop. 'I'd like a nice pair of **crocodile** shoes please,' she said.

'Certainly, madam,' said the assistant. *'What size shoes does the crocodile take?!'*

A drink for my **crocodile** please, and make it snappy!

CURTAINS
Why should you always take a pencil up to bed with you?
*So you can draw the **curtains**, of course!*

Doctor, doctor, I think I'm a pair of **curtains**.
Well, pull yourself together then!

What did one **curtain** say to the other one?
Well, I'll be hanged!

D

DAD

A girl came home from school and her **dad**
asked if she'd had her homework marked.
'Yes, Dad,' she replied. *'I'm afraid you didn't do
very well!'*

SMALL BOY: My mum often calls my **dad**
'wonder man'. She says it's because she
sometimes wonders if he's a man!

DANCE

What **dance** can you do in the bathroom?
A tap dance!

ADVERT:
**THE TUMBLEOVA SCHOOL
OF DANCING**

COME TO THE
FAMOUS TUMBLEOVA
SCHOOL OF DANCING
LEARN TO DO
THE ANCIENT SCOTTISH
SWORD DANCE
THEN YOU CAN DANCE AND
CUT YOUR TOE-NAILS AT THE
SAME TIME!

Where do snowmen go to **dance**?
A snowball.

DID YOU HEAR ABOUT THE IDIOTIC MORRIS DANCER?

NO, WHAT ABOUT HIM?

HE FELL OFF THE BONNET!

DARTS

A man went into a pub with his dog and ordered a drink. Then he and the dog started playing **darts**! 'Hey, that's amazing!' said the barman. 'Your dog can play darts!'

'It's not that amazing,' replied the man. '*In the last ten games he's only beaten me twice!*'

DEER

What do you call a **deer** with no eyes?
No eye deer!

What do you call a **deer** with no eyes and no legs?
Still no eye deer!!

DENTIST

What's the difference between a wet day and a boy at the **dentist's**?
One pours with rain, the other roars with pain.

Carol's mum had just taken her to the **dentist** because she had a toothache. On the way home they dropped in on Carol's gran for a cup of tea. 'Is your tooth still hurting, dear?' asked the elderly lady, kindly.

'*I don't know,*' replied Carol. '*The dentist kept it!*'

DESERT
Why does a lion in the **desert** remind you of Christmas?
Because of his sandy claws!

What do you call a snowman in a **desert**?
A wet patch in the sand!

DIAMONDS
A mean man's girl friend said to him: 'Oh, darling, please buy me something with **diamonds** in it for my birthday.'
'*O K,*' said the man, '*How about a pack of cards?*'

DIET
FAT MAN: I'm on a special sea-food **diet**.
HIS FRIEND: Are you?
FAT MAN: *Yes, I only have to see food and I eat it!*

A teacher was talking to a new girl on her first day of school.
'What are you going to be when you're grown up like your mummy?'
'*On a diet,*' said the girl.

DINNER
What's the difference between school **dinner** and pig swill?
School dinners come on a plate.

Mummy, Mummy, what's for **dinner**?
Shut up, and get back in the oven!

Knock knock!
Who's there?
Bernadette.
Bernadette who?
*Bernadette my **dinner**!*

DINNER LADY

HANG ON-THERE'S NOTHING FUNNY ABOUT DINNER LADIES!

YES, THERE IS. DIDN'T YOU HEAR ABOUT THE DINNER LADY WHO GOT AN ELECTRIC SHOCK? SHE STOOD ON A BUN AND A CURRANT SHOT UP HER LEG!

DINNER MONEY
Have you heard about the little boy on his first day at school?
He took his **dinner money** *and ate it*!

DINOSAURS
A boy was walking down the high street when he saw a huge **dinosaur** looking in a shop window. The boy put a long string round the dinosaur's neck and led him down the road to the police station. 'I've just found this stray dinosaur,' the boy said to a policeman on duty there. 'What should I do with him?'

'I think you should take him to the museum,' said the policeman. The next day the policeman was on point duty in the town when he saw the boy and the dinosaur walking down the street towards him.

'Hey, I thought I told you to take that dinosaur to the museum,' said the officer.

'I did,' said the boy. '*And today we are going to the cinema!*'

DISMAY

Knock knock!
Who's there?
Dismay.
Dismay who?
Dismay surprise you!

DOCTORS

Doctor, doctor, everyone ignores me.
Next!

Doctor, doctor, I've only got fifty-nine seconds to live!
Sit over there, I'll see you in a minute.

Doctor, doctor, I'm at death's door.
Don't worry, I'll pull you through!

Doctor, doctor, I've gone cricket crazy.
How's that?
Not out!

PUBLIC ANNOUNCEMENT:
NEVER ARGUE WITH YOUR DOCTOR,
HE HAS INSIDE INFORMATION!

Doctor, doctor, my wife thinks she's a swallow.
Tell her to come and see me.
I can't, she's flown south for the winter!

DOGS

What do trees and **dogs** have in common?
Bark!

A man went into his kitchen and saw his **dog** sitting in the frying pan.
   'What are you doing in there?' he asked.
   'I'm a sausage dog,' replied the dog.

How do you stop a **dog** digging up your garden?
Take away his spade!

A man went into a pub with a poodle on a lead. 'This **dog** is a police dog,' he said to a friend.

'Really?' replied the friend. 'It doesn't look much like a police dog.'

'*I know*,' said the man. '*It works in the plain clothes division!*'

Doctor, doctor, I think I'm a **dog**.
Sit down and tell me all about it.
I can't.
Why not?
I'm not allowed on the furniture!

POLICEMAN: Has this **dog** got a licence?
BOY: *No, he doesn't need one – he's too young to drive.*

What breed of **dog** has no tail?
A hot dog!

FASCINATING FACT: A sheep **dog** is cheaper to keep than a golden retriever because you only need a black and white licence.

DOLL

A small girl rushed to her mother: 'Mummy, Mummy, Jimmie has broken my **doll**.'

'How did it happen?'

'When I hit him with it her head fell off!'

DOOR

When is a **door** not a door?
When it's ajar!

A boy went into the back garden and spoke to his mother: 'A man came to the **door**, Mum. He said he was collecting for the Children's Home.'

'Did you give him something?'

'Yes, my baby sister.'

There's a lady at the **door** with a pram.
Tell her to push off!

DOUBLE VISION

A lady went to the doctor and complained that her eyesight didn't seem quite right. He inspected her and said: 'You've got **double vision**.'

'Don't be daft,' said the lady. *'I'm not taking any notice of you two!'*

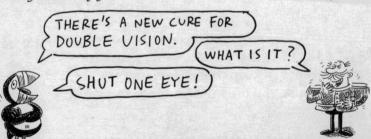

DOWN

How do you get **down** from an elephant?
You don't, *you get down from a duck!*

What goes up but never comes **down**?
Your age!

DRACULA

DRACULA IS A PAIN IN THE NECK!

IF YOU FELL IN LOVE WITH HIM, WOULD IT BE LOVE AT FIRST BITE?!

ADVERT:
IF YOU LIKE DRACULA
JOIN HIS FANG CLUB!

DRESS

LADY: Can I try on that **dress** in the window?
SHOP ASSISTANT: *I'd use a changing-room if I were you, madam!'*

DRIVING LESSONS

ADVERT:
TRY MR PRANG'S SPECIAL
CRASH COURSE IN DRIVING

YOU'LL HAVE A BUMPER NUMBER OF ACCIDENTS!

DROWNING

'Help!' shouted a man in the middle of a river. 'I'm **drowning**, I can't swim!'

'*So what,*' said a man on the bank. '*I can't play the violin, but I don't make a fuss about it!*'

DRUM

There's a man at the door with a **drum**. *Tell him to beat it!*

DUCKS

> **FASCINATING FACT:** There's nothing a **duck** likes better than to put its webbed feet up, open a box of Cream Quackers and watch a duckumentary on TV.

THEY LIKE THE FEATHER FORECAST TOO!

ANY GREAT JOKES MAKE THEM QUACK UP!

DUSTMAN

Never ask a **dustman** how his business is going. He'll say it's 'picking up'!

E

EARS

TELL ME, FAT PUFFIN, WHAT KIND OF EARS DOES AN ENGINE HAVE?

I DON'T KNOW

ENGINEERS!

IN THAT CASE MOUNTAINS MUST HAVE MOUNTAINEERS!

EARWIGS

FASCINATING FACT: When **earwigs** go to a football match they all chant 'Earwigo-earwigo-earwigo!'

EGGS

'Waiter, these **eggs** are horrible.' 'Don't blame me, sir, *I only lay the tables!*'

* Old *
Chestnut
Award

Two **eggs** were sitting in a pan full of boiling water.

'Corr . . .' said the first egg. 'This is terrible – it's so hot in here!'

'*This is nothing,*' replied the other. '*When you get taken out someone sits you in a little cup and bashes your head in!*'

How do ghosts like their **eggs** cooked?
Petrified!

EGYPT

Why was the **Egyptian** boy looking so sad?
Because his daddy was a mummy!

EIFFEL TOWER

GIRL: I can jump as high as the **Eiffel Tower**.
HER FRIEND: I bet you can't.
GIRL: *I can you know – the Eiffel Tower can't jump!*

▷ **see Empire State Building joke on page 56**

ELECTRICIAN

An **electrician** went to the pub and when he came home his friend said: '*Wire you insulate?*'

I'VE GOT IT – WHY ARE YOU IN SO LATE!

ELEPHANTS

THANK HEAVENS FOR **ELEPHANTS**—OTHERWISE HOW COULD YOU FIND ENOUGH JOKES FOR THE LETTER **E** IN THE GREAT PUFFIN JOKE DIRECTORY!

How do you know if there's an **elephant** in your fridge?
Footprints in the butter!

How do you know if there's an **elephant** in your bed?
Your nose touches the ceiling!

How do you know if there's an **elephant** in your pudding?
Very lumpy custard!

Why is an **elephant** so wrinkled?
Have you ever tried to iron an elephant?

ELEPHANTS HAVE WRINKLED FEET TO GIVE MICE A CHANCE!

What is as big as an **elephant** but doesn't weigh anything?
An elephant's shadow.

Two **elephants** went on holiday and sat down on the beach. It was a very hot day and they fancied having a swim in the sea. Unfortunately they couldn't: *they only had one pair of trunks!*

▷ see **Holiday jokes** on page 84

What would you get if you crossed an **elephant** with a kangaroo?
Holes in Australia.

OR SOME VERY FLAT AUSTRALIANS!

An **elephant's** ghost is an elephantom!

ELIZABETH
Elizabeth II Rules – UK!

EMPIRE STATE BUILDING
What's big and black and hairy and climbs up the **Empire State Building** in a party frock?
Queen Kong!

ENVELOPE
What did the stamp say to the **envelope**?
Stick with me and we'll go places!

ESKIMOS
How does an **Eskimo** keep the roof on his house?
'E glues it!!

When **Eskimos** go shopping, do they buy things with iced lolly?

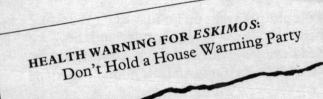

HEALTH WARNING FOR *ESKIMOS*:
Don't Hold a House Warming Party

IS AN ESKIMO'S COW CALLED AN ESKIMOO?

EXAGGERATE

ANGRY FATHER: I've told you a million times not to **exaggerate**!

EXAMS

'Please, sir, I've finished the **exam**,' said a girl. 'Good,' said the teacher. 'Did the questions give you any difficulties?'

'No,' she replied, '*but some of the answers did!*'

EXAMS – RESULTS OF

A boy came home from school with his **exam** results.

'How did you get on, son?' asked his father.
'My marks were under water,' said the boy.
'What do you mean "under water"?'
'They were all below "C" level!'

'I've got some good news for you about my **exam** results,' said a girl coming home from school.

'What do you mean?' said her parents.
'Well, you know you said you'd give me ten pounds for every exam I passed – *I've just saved you a lot of money!'*

EXECUTIONERS

FASCINATING FACT: In the olden days executioners knew who to execute because they had a chopping list.

EXITS

PLEASE NOTE – THERE IS NOTHING FUNNY ABOUT EXITS: THEY ARE ON THE WAY OUT !

EYE

What did one **eye** say to the other eye?
Between you and me something smells.

YES – A NOSE !

EYE TEST

A small girl was having an **eye test**. 'Can you read out the letters on the chart on the wall?' asked the optician.

'*What chart?*' replied the girl.

HAVE YOUR EYES EVER BEEN CHECKED, FAT PUFFIN ?

NO, THEY'VE ALWAYS BEEN PLAIN YELLOW!

F

FARMERS

Did you hear about the **farmer** who ploughed his field with a steamroller? *He wanted to grow mashed potatoes!*

A **farmer** decided that it would be a good idea to try to breed turkeys with three legs – he thought they would be very popular at Christmas time. He spent months and months working on the problem, and finally he was successful.

'It's fantastic!' he said to a friend. 'I've managed to breed turkeys with three legs!'

'How amazing!' said the friend. 'Do they taste any good?'

'I don't know,' said the farmer. '*I haven't managed to catch one yet!*'

FIRST **FARMER**: You know when I told you that my cow was sick you said give it liquid paraffin to drink.

SECOND FARMER: Yes, that's what I gave to mine.

FIRST FARMER: Well, my cow just died.

SECOND FARMER: *So did mine!*

What group of heroes protects **farmers**?
The Hay Team!

FARMERS' CHILDREN GO TO SCHOOL TO TAKE HAY LEVELS!

FASHION

NEWSFLASH:
Some **fashion** news has just come in from Paris.
Skirts and dresses will be the same length as last year, but legs will be longer.

FATHER CHRISTMAS

FIRST CHILD: What nationality is **Father Christmas**?
SECOND CHILD: *North Pole-ish?*

this way to Santa jokes on page 149

FEET

How many **feet** in a yard?
It depends how many people are standing in it!

What wears shoes but has no **feet**?
A pavement.

What's the last thing you take off at night before going to bed?
Your **feet** – *you take them off the floor and put them in the bed!*

FELIX

Knock knock!
Who's there?
Felix.
Felix who?
Felix my lolly once more I'll belt him!

HE'S A SUCKER!

FENCING

Did you hear about the idiotic Olympic **fencing** team? *They ran out of Creosote!*

FIRE

Did you hear about the plastic surgeon who got too close to the **fire**?
He melted.

FIREMEN

What were the two Spanish **firemen** called?
Hosé and Hose B!

FIR TREE

What do you call a girl with a **fir tree** on her head?
Christmas Carol!

OH, I SEE – NO 'I's!

FISH

What do you call **fish** with no eyes?
F-SSSSHHHH!

What kind of **fish** can't swim?
A dead one!

What **fish** swims at a hundred miles an hour?
A motorpike!

What **fish** sleep a lot?
Kippers!

FISH AND CHIPS

A man went into a **fish and chip** shop and said: 'Fish and chips twice!'

'It's all right,' said the man behind the counter. '*I heard you the first time!*'

A man came out of a **fish and chip** shop and stood by a bus stop eating his supper out of the paper. A woman with a small yappy dog arrived, and the dog kept pestering the man for some food.

'Can I throw him a bit?' the man asked the woman.

'Sure,' she replied.

So the man bent down, picked up the dog and threw it over a wall!

FISHING

Two not very bright gentlemen rented a rowing boat and went **fishing** on a lake. Suddenly they started to catch quite a lot of fish. 'This bit of the lake is good for fishing. Put a mark on the side of the boat so we'll be able to find the same spot again,' said one of them.

'*Don't be daft,*' said the other, '*we might not get the same boat next time!*'

FISHMONGER

'Please would you clean these fish for me, **fishmonger**,' asked a lady.

'Certainly, madam,' replied the fishmonger. *'I'll put them in the automatic fishwasher.'*

FLAMINGOS

TEACHER: Why do **flamingos** stand with one leg out of the water?

SMALL GIRL: *If they took both legs out they'd fall in it!*

FLEA

FIRST FLEA: How are you?

SECOND FLEA: Not very well – *I'm not feeling up to scratch!*

I HEARD ABOUT A DOG THAT WENT TO A FLEA CIRCUS AND STOLE THE SHOW!

WELL, I KNOW HOW TO START A FLEA RACE. YOU SAY: ONE TWO FLEA GO!

FLIES

Two **flies** were playing football in a saucer. *They were practising for the cup!*

Doctor, doctor, I keep thinking I'm a **fly**. *Well buzz off then.*

Waiter, what's this **fly** doing in my soup? *Breaststroke, sir!*

★ Old ★ Chestnut Award

'WAITER, THERE'S A FLY IN MY SOUP' IS ONE OF THE WORLD'S OLDEST AND BEST JOKES. THERE ARE SO MANY REPLIES THE WAITER CAN GIVE! HERE ARE JUST A FEW OF THEM:

'Yes, he's committed insecticide, sir.'

'Don't worry, he won't live long in that stuff!'

'It's hardly deep enough to drown him, sir.'

'They don't seem to care what they eat, sir!'

'Shall I give him the kiss of life, sir?'

'Sorry, no pets allowed in here.'

'Don't worry, there's no extra charge, sir.'

'Don't make a fuss or everyone will want one.'

'I'll fetch him a spoon, sir.'

'So that's where they go in the winter!'

FLOWERS

Flowers Rule – Bouquet!

What did the bee say to the **flower**?
Hello, honey!

FOG

I CALL MY CAT 'FOG'.

WHY?

BECAUSE HE'S GREY AND THICK!

FOOD MIXER

BOY'S FATHER: Have you got something for
Mum for her birthday, son?
BOY: Yes, I've bought her a new **food mixer**.
FATHER: A food mixer! How ever did you afford
that?!
BOY: *Well, it's only a wooden spoon.*

FOOTBALL

A boy was very late for school. 'Why are you so
late?' said the Head Teacher sternly.

'I'm sorry,' said the boy. 'I was dreaming
about **football**.'

'And why does dreaming about football make
you late for school?'

'*They played extra time!*' said the boy.

FIRST LADY: My son has got into the school **football** team.
SECOND LADY: What position does he play in?
FIRST LADY: *He's left back in the dressing room!*

TELL ME, MAJOR, WHY IS IT SO COLD AT FOOTBALL MATCHES?

I DON'T KNOW.

I THINK IT'S BECAUSE THERE ARE SO MANY FANS!

When it stops rolling, does a **football** look round?

FOOTBALL SHORTS

A boy came home from school and told his father: 'My teacher says I need a new pair of **football shorts** for gym.'

'*Tell her Jim will have to get his own football shorts!*'

FOOT PUMP

ADVERT: Buy Our Famous Foot Pumps Ideal If You've Got Flat Feet!

FORGETFUL

I CAN'T REMEMBER IF I USED TO BE FORGETFUL!

FORK

Did you hear about the man who got a puncture because there was a **fork** in the road?

FORTUNE

How can you get a small **fortune**?
Start with a big one and spend most of it!

FOSSILS

NEWSFLASH:
Archaeologists have found the **fossils** of a one-eyed dinosaur; they are going to call it a *Do-you-think-he-saw-us!*

FOX

What do you get if you cross a **fox** with a chicken?
A fox!

FOX HOUND

What is a **fox hound's** favourite food?
Fox tail soup!

FREE SPEECH

A man was sitting in a restaurant and he called the waitress over. 'Excuse me, waitress, do you believe in **free speech**?' he asked.

'Of course I do,' said the waitress.

'*Good*,' replied the man. '*I'll use your telephone!*'

FRIDGE

If a **fridge** could sing, would it sing 'Freeze a jolly good fellow'?

FROGS

What's a **frog's** favourite drink?
Croakacola!

I THOUGHT IT WAS HOT CROAKO!

Where do **frogs** go to the toilet?
A croakroom!

Doctor, doctor, I think I'm a **frog**.
Well, I can't see you now – hop it!

What do you call a girl with a **frog** on her head?
Lily!

69

What happens if a **frog's** car breaks down?
It gets toad away!

How did the **frog** die?
It Kermitted suicide!

FROGS' LEGS

MAN IN RESTAURANT: Waiter –
do you have **frogs' legs**?
WAITER: No, sir, *I've always walked like this!*

Or this one:

MAN IN RESTAURANT: Waiter, do you have
frogs' legs?
WAITER: Yes, sir.
MAN: *Well hop off to the kitchen and get me a steak!*

FUR

TEACHER: Can you get **fur** from skunks?
SMALL BOY: Yes, Miss, *as fur as possible!*

FUTURE

A man went to the doctor's. 'It's amazing, I
think I can see into the **future**,' he said.
   'When did this start?' asked the doctor.
   '*Next Wednesday*,' said the man.

G

GAMBLING

What do you call a lady who likes **gambling**?
Betty!

GAME

What **game** do horses like best?
Stable tennis!

GARDENER

Why did the **gardener** plant bulbs?
So that the worms could see where they were going!

I GET IT – LIGHT BULBS !

THAT'S RIGHT. GARDENERS NEED A SENSE OF HUMOUS !

GARDENING

A vicar was walking down a lane in the village
when he came to a cottage where an old man
was doing some **gardening**.

'Your garden looks very nice, Mr Giles,' said
the vicar. 'It's wonderful what God can do with
a little help.'

'Huh!' said the old man. '*You should see the
mess He made of it when He had it to himself!*'

GCSE

What do you call a boy with nineteen **GCSEs**?
A liar!

GHOSTS

What is a **ghost's** favourite food?
Spookghetti!

What else?
Ghoulash!

I WONDER IF GHOSTS BELIEVE IN PEOPLE?

GIRAFFE

FASCINATING FACT: Its neck is so long that a **giraffe** has to stand on a chair to clean its teeth.

WHAT DO YOU GET IF YOU CROSS A GIRAFFE WITH A HEDGEHOG?

A FIVE METRE HAIRBRUSH!

I DON'T KNOW.

AH, BUT IF YOU CROSS A GIRAFFE WITH AN ALSATIAN DOG YOU GET AN ANIMAL THAT BITES LOW-FLYING AIRCRAFT!

GIRL FRIEND

FIRST BOY: My **girl friend** has the face of a saint.
SECOND BOY: Really?
FIRST BOY: *Yes, a Saint Bernard!*

GLASSES

Doctor, doctor, I think I need **glasses**.
You certainly do, *this is a fish and chip shop!*

GLOW WORMS

FASCINATING FACT: **Glow worms'** children
are not very bright!

GEORGE MICHAEL SINGS ABOUT
GLOW WORMS - 'WAKE ME UP BEFORE
YOU GLOW GLOW!'

What is a **glow worm's** favourite food?
Anything, so long as it's just a light snack!

GNOMES

Did you hear about the sick **gnome**? It went to
the Elf Centre.

'Where did you get all these gnomes from?'
'I bought them at the Ideal **Gnome** Exhibition.'

I THOUGHT HE MIGHT HAVE GOT THEM
FROM THE NATIONAL ELF SERVICE!

GOATS

HERE IS THE OLDEST JOKE IN THE HISTORY OF THE ENTIRE WORLD:

Doctor, doctor, I think I'm a **goat**!
How long have you felt like this?
Since I was a kid!

★ Old ★ Chestnut Award

THIS ONE ONLY GOES BACK TO ABOUT 1066:

I've got a **goat** in my bedroom.
The smell must be terrible!
He's getting used to it!!!

GOATS ARE ALWAYS BUTTING IN!

GOLDFISH

'Mary, have you changed the water in the **goldfish** bowl as I asked you?'
'No, they haven't drunk this lot yet.'

GOLF

Why do people who play **golf** need a spare pair of shoes?
In case they get a hole in one!

GORILLAS

Why don't **gorillas** like penguins?
They can't get the wrappers off!

GOWN

A lady went into a shop and said: 'I'd like a beautiful ball **gown**, in a colour that will match my eyes.'

'I'm sorry, madam,' said the assistant. '*We don't have anything in bloodshot!*'

GRAFFITI

FIRST MAN: Do you like **graffiti**?

SECOND MAN: *No, I don't like any Italian food!*

GRAMMAR

A teacher called to see a small girl's mother about her work at school. 'I want to speak to your mother, dear,' said the teacher.

'She ain't here,' replied the girl.

'*Isn't*, not "ain't",' the teacher corrected her. 'Where's your **grammar**?'

'*She ain't here either*,' said the girl.

WHICH BRINGS US TO:

GRANDFATHER CLOCK

A man was staggering down the road carrying a huge **grandfather clock** on his back. 'Excuse me,' said a little old lady. 'Can you tell me what time it is?'

Another man was staggering down *another* road with a huge **grandfather clock** on his back. As he turned a corner the base of it hit *another* little old lady and nearly knocked her over.

  '*Why can't you wear a wrist-watch like everyone else!*' she said crossly.

GRANNIES

'My **granny** hasn't got a grey hair on her head.'

  'Really?'

  '*Yes, she's completely bald!*'

'My **granny** has teeth like stars.'

  'Really?'

  '*Yes – they come out at night!*'

GRAPE

What did the **grape** say
when the elephant stood
on it?
*Nothing, it just gave out
a little whine!*

GRAPEFRUIT

What's yellow and never needs ironing?
*A drip-dry **grapefruit**!*

GRASSHOPPER

MAN IN RESTAURANT: Waiter, there's a
grasshopper in my soup!
WAITER: Yes, sir, *it's the fly's day off!*

GRAVESTONES

GRAVITY

WHAT STOPPED PEOPLE FALLING
OFF THE EARTH BEFORE THEY PASSED
THE LAW OF GRAVITY?

GRECIAN URN

What's a **Grecian urn?**
About a hundred quid a week!

GREEN

GREEN AND YELLOW ARE UNDOUBTEDLY THE TWO JOKIEST COLOURS.

▷ **see Yellow jokes on page 187!**

What's **green** and jumps round the garden?
A spring onion!

What's **green** and hairy
and goes up and down?
A gooseberry in a lift!

★Old★
Chestnut
Award

What's **green** and brown and if it jumped out of
a tree on to you it would kill you?
A billiard table!

What's **green** and noisy?
A froghorn!

◁ **see page 69 for Frog jokes!**

Who's **green** and holds up stage coaches?
Dick Gherkin.

GREENFLY

GREY

What's **grey** with four legs and a trunk?
A mouse going on holiday!

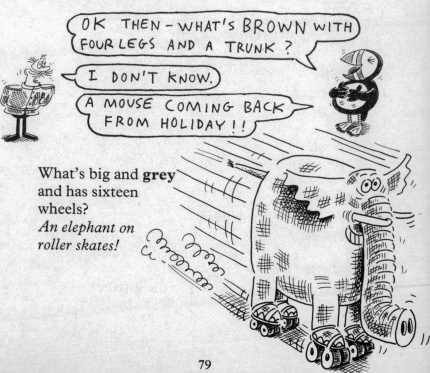

OK THEN – WHAT'S BROWN WITH FOUR LEGS AND A TRUNK?

I DON'T KNOW.

A MOUSE COMING BACK FROM HOLIDAY!!

What's big and **grey** and has sixteen wheels?
An elephant on roller skates!

79

What's **grey** with a red scarf and check trousers?
Rupert the Elephant!

A little girl asked her mum why she had some
grey hairs.
   'Probably because you're so naughty to me,'
joked her mum.
   '*You must have been horrible to granny then!*'
said the girl.

GROCER
A girl went into a **grocer's** shop. 'Can I have a
pound of apples and two wasps, please?' she
asked.
   'I'm sorry, we don't sell wasps,' said the
grocer.
   'Well,' said the girl, 'why have you got some
in your window?'

GUESS
Knock knock!
Who's there?
Guess!
Guess who?
No, you guess who!

GUM TREES
What lives in **gum trees**?
Stick insects!

GUTTER
What's big and red, and lies in the **gutter**?
A dead bus!

H

HAIR

Doctor, doctor, my **hair** keeps falling out, can
you give me something to keep it in?
Yes, here's a paper bag.

Why did the bald man go outside?
*To get some fresh **hair**!*

When can you dive into a barrel of water without
getting your **hair** wet?
When you're bald.

HALIBUT

A man walked into a restaurant. 'Do you serve
halibut?' he asked.

'Yes, sir,' said the waiter. '*Sit down, we serve
anybody!*'

HANDS

What can you put in your left **hand** but not
your right?
Your right elbow!

MAJOR - WHAT HAS HANDS BUT
NEVER WASHES ITS FACE?

A CLOCK!

HARES

When do **hares** have eight legs?
When there are two of them!

HAT

What did the **hat** say to the tie?
You hang around while I go on ahead!

HEAD

FASCINATING FACT: No one can stand on their **head** – their feet aren't high up enough!

HEAD TEACHER

A boy came home to his mother: 'Our **Head Teacher** has converted me to religion.'

'Really, dear?' said his mother, impressed.

'Yes, I didn't believe in hell until I went to her school!'

HEDGEHOG

What's a **hedgehog's** favourite food?
Prickled onions!

I GET THE GIGGLES IF I EAT TICKLED ONIONS!

What do you get if you cross a **hedgehog** with a sheep?
An animal that knits its own sweaters!

HEIDI

Knock knock!
Who's there?
Heidi.
Heidi who?
No, Hi di hi!

HENS

WATCH OUT – THESE MAY BE CHICKEN JOKES IN DISGUISE!

A man was driving his car along a lane past a cottage when a **hen** ran out into the road. The man ran over it and killed it. Like a good chap he stopped the car and knocked on the cottage door.

'I'm terribly sorry, but I've just run over one of your hens,' he said to the lady who opened the door. 'I'd like to replace it.'

'OK,' said the lady. '*How many eggs do you lay a week?*'

LADY (on phone to doctor): Doctor, I'm very worried, my husband keeps thinking he's turned into a **hen**.
DOCTOR: Why didn't you tell me this before?
LADY: Well, *we've needed the eggs!*

ANGRY FARMER: You've run over one of my **hens**!

MOTORIST: Yes, *it's a flat battery hen!*

HEROES

Who is the daftest **hero**?
Prattman!

HIJACK

NEWSFLASH:
The **hijack** at the zoo is over. The police have shot the gorillas and released all their hostridges.

HIPPOPOTAMUS

A lady took her little son to a museum. They walked round and after a while came to a huge glass case with a stuffed **hippopotamus** inside it.

'Mummy,' asked the boy, *'how did they shoot it without breaking the glass?'*

HOLIDAY

How do elephants go on **holiday**?
They travel by Jumbo jet!

OR MAYBE BY ELECOPTER!

Where do they go?
Tuskany!

for other Elephant jokes see page 55

Where do ghosts go for their **holidays**?
The Isle of Fright!

THEY GO THERE BY BRITISH SCAREWAYS!

HOMEWORK

CAN YOU COME OUT TO PLAY?

NO, I'M HELPING DAD WITH MY HOMEWORK.

A class were doing a project on food, and Ann was told to make a list for **homework** of six things that contain milk.
She wrote: *Rice pudding, milk chocolate and four cows!*

HONEY

Why do bees have sticky hair?
*Because they have **honey** combs.*

HORSE

How do you hire a **horse**?
Stand it on four bricks!

I CAN PROVE THAT A HORSE HAS TEN LEGS.

GO ON THEN.

IT HAS TWO FORELEGS, THAT MAKES EIGHT LEGS, BECAUSE TWO FOURS ARE EIGHT, PLUS TWO BACK LEGS, THAT MAKES TEN!

HORSE RACING

A man was sitting on his sofa reading a **horse racing** newspaper while his baby daughter played on the floor in front of him.

'Baby's nose is running again,' he said to his wife.

'*Don't you ever think about anything except racing!*' she replied.

HOSANNA

Knock knock!
Who's there?
Hosanna.
Hosanna who?
Hosanna Claus going to get to my stocking, we haven't got a chimney!?

HOT DOG

GIRL: My new boy friend is a terrible snob.
HER FRIEND: Really?
GIRL: Yes, he won't buy a **hot dog** unless it's got a pedigree!

HOUSE

A man was asking an estate agent about a **house** he wanted to buy.

'Does the roof leak?' he asked.

'Only when it rains,' said the agent.

HUMAN CANNON-BALL

Did you hear about the **human cannon-ball** who lost his job?

They fired him.

HUMPTY

Question: What did **Humpty** do with his hat?

Answer: Humpty *dumped his hat on a wall*!

HYENA

A **hyena** ate a box of Oxo cubes and made a laughing stock of itself!

IF YOU CROSS A HYENA WITH A PARROT YOU GET AN ANIMAL THAT LAUGHS AT ITS OWN JOKES!

I

ICE-CREAM
What football team
sounds like **ice-cream**?
Aston Vanilla!

THAT'S RIGHT, AND
THEY ALWAYS
GET LICKED!

ICE LOLLY
Doctor, doctor, I feel like an **ice lolly**.
So do I, bring me one please!

IGUANA
Knock knock!
Who's there?
Iguana.
Iguana who?
Iguana hold your hand!

ILLNESS
A small boy came back from school looking very
pleased with himself. 'What's the matter with
you?' asked his mother, jokingly.
    'Our school may have to close because of
illness,' he said.
    'Whatever do you mean?' asked his mother
again.
    'The teachers say they are sick of us!'

INDIAN
What's the difference between an **Indian**
elephant and an African elephant?
About three thousand miles!

INFLUENZA

HE WAS AN INTRUDER — HE CAME IN-TRU—DER WINDER!

INVISIBLE MAN
Doctor, doctor, I keep thinking I'm the **Invisible Man**.
Well I can't see you now.

WERE THE INVISIBLE MAN'S MOTHER AND FATHER HIS TRANS-PARENTS?

I SAY I SAY I SAY!
I say, I say, I say, did you hear about the optician whose trousers fell down? He made a spectacle of himself!

IN THE OLDEN DAYS, JUST AFTER THE DINOSAURS HAD LEFT THE EARTH AND YOUR DAD STILL WORE SHORT TROUSERS, ALL JOKES BEGAN WITH 'I SAY I SAY I SAY!'

ISLAND

Three men were stuck on a desert **island** and a
fairy came along and offered them a free wish
each.

'I wish I was back with my family and friends,'
said the first man, and in the twinkling of an eye
he disappeared back home.

'I too wish I was back with my family and
friends,' said the next man, and he too
disappeared.

'It's very lonely here,' said the last man. '*I
wish my two friends were here with me . . .!*'

J

JAGUAR

FIRST MAN: You know old Fred's wife said she wanted a **Jaguar**.

SECOND MAN: Yes.

FIRST MAN: Well he bought her one.

SECOND MAN: Really? What happened?

FIRST MAN: *It ate her!*

> **FASCINATING FACT:** The fastest animal on earth is the E-type **Jaguar**.

JAM

What **jam** do traffic wardens like?
Traffic jam.

What's big and grey, sits in a river, and squirts **jam** at you?
A hippopotamus eating a doughnut.

JAMAICA

MAN: My wife is going to the West Indies.

HIS FRIEND: **Jamaica?**

MAN: *No, she's going of her own accord!*

* Old *
Chestnut
Award

THAT REMINDS ME. MY WIFE WENT TO INDONESIA.

JAKARTA?

NO, SHE WENT BY AEROPLANE!

JAM SANDWICH

COOKERY TEACHER: Jane, what's the most obvious thing to put into a **jam sandwich**?
JANE: *Your teeth!*

JEEP

Two men in a **jeep** were motoring along across the grasslands of Africa. Two lions lay beneath some scrubby bushes near the track ahead of them. 'Look,' said the first lion, *'meals on wheels!'*

JELLY

How do you start a **jelly** race?
Get set!

▷ **see page 165 for how to start a Teddy Bear race!**

What do you get if you cross a **jelly** with a sheep dog?
Colliewobbles!

A man was sitting on a park bench with a **jelly** in one ear and some fruit in the other.
   A boy went up to him and said: 'Excuse me, but you've got a jelly in one ear and some fruit in the other.'
   'You'll have to speak up,' said the man. *'I'm a trifle deaf.'*

JEWELLER

What's the difference between a **jeweller** and a jailer?
One sells watches, the other watches cells!

JOHN

What did St **John** say when he tried to teach St Luke road safety?
Stop, Luke, and listen!

JOKES

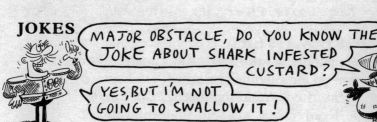

MAJOR OBSTACLE, DO YOU KNOW THE JOKE ABOUT SHARK INFESTED CUSTARD?

YES, BUT I'M NOT GOING TO SWALLOW IT!

Have you heard the **joke** about the brick wall?
No.
I won't tell it to you, *you'd never get over it*!

Have you heard the **joke** about the quick sand?
No.
It will take a long time to sink in.

Do you know the **joke** about chicken-pox?
No.
I won't tell it to you, *you'd only go and pass it on*!

Do you know the **joke** about the broken pencil?
No.
I won't tell it to you, *there's no point to it*!

I KNOW A JOKE ABOUT BUTTER, BUT I'M NOT GOING TO SPREAD IT!

I KNOW ONE ABOUT A DUSTBIN, BUT IT'S ABSOLUTE RUBBISH!

Knock knock!
Who's there?
Boo.
Boo who?
*There's no need to cry, it's only a **joke**!*

JOKE WRITER

A man met a **joke writer** at a party. 'What do you do for a living?' he asked.

'I write jokes for children.'

'Really, have you sold anything yet?'

'Yes. My TV, car, and the family silver.'

J.R.

What gum does **J.R.** use?

Ewing Gum!

see another Chewing Gum joke on page 35.

JUMBO

What's big and grey and mumbles?

*A mumbo-**jumbo**!*

JUNGLES

A huge lion was swaggering through the **jungle** when he met a mouse. 'Why is it . . .' asked the lion, 'that I am such a grand, masterly creature, fierce and brave, and you, little mouse, are so puny and small and weedy?'

'Well, I've been rather ill recently,' replied the mouse.

Why shouldn't you play cards in the **jungle**?

There are too many cheetahs!

What's white and fluffy and swings through the
jungle?
A meringue-ootang.

What do you call a polar bear in a **jungle**?
Lost!

JUNK SHOP
A man went into a **junk shop** and asked the
man behind the counter: 'Is this a second-hand
shop?'

'Yes,' said the shopkeeper.

'Good,' replied the man. *'Then you can fit one
to my grandfather clock!'*

JUNO
Knock knock!
Who's there?
Juno.
Juno who?
*Juno how long I've been waiting for you to open
this door?*

K

KANGAROO

What do you get if you cross
a sheep with a **kangaroo**?
A woolly jumper!

★Old ★
Chestnut
Award

Kangaroo's Birthday Card:
Many Hoppy Returns!

FASCINATING FACT: Mother **kangaroos**
get very annoyed if their children eat
biscuits in bed!

KERMIT

Where does **Kermit** keep his money?
In a Miss Piggy Bank!

KETTLE

'John, go and put the
kettle on, there's a
good boy,' said John's
mother.
  '*I don't think it will
fit me, Mum,*' he replied.

KEYS

What **keys** scratch themselves under the arms?
Monkeys!

KEYS – CAR

A man was phoning a garage: 'Please come
quickly, I've shut my car **keys** in my sports car.
*Hurry, I've left the roof open and it's starting to
rain!'*

KING

Where does the **king** keep his armies?
Up his sleevies!

KISS

BOY: My darling, what would I have to give you
to get a little **kiss**?
GIRL: *An anaesthetic!*

KLEPTOMANIA

What can I take for KLEPTOMANIA?

KNIFE

What do you call a man with a **knife** on his
head?
Stanley!

KNIGHTS

Where do **knights** learn how to fight?
At knight school of course!

What is a **knight's** favourite Christmas carol?
Silent knight!

KNITTING

A lady was driving very fast down the road in a sports car. A policeman watched her go past and noticed that as well as driving she was **knitting**! He leapt on to his motorbike and chased her. When he got alongside her car he leant over and said, 'Pull over!'

'*No,*' shouted back the lady. '*A scarf!*'

KNOCK KNOCKS!

Knock knock!
Who's there?
Ivor.
Ivor who?
Ivor you open the door or I knock it down!

Knock knock!
Who's there?
Tish.
Tish who?
Bless You!

Knock knock!
Who's there?
Dorabella.
Dorabella who?
Dorabella not working so I had to knock!

Knock knock!
Who's there?
Wendy.
Wendy who?
Wendy heck are you going to let me in!

Knock knock!
Who's there?
Twitter.
Twitter who?
I didn't know you did owl impressions!

Knock knock!
Who's there?
Micky.
Micky who?
Micky won't fit, that's why I'm knocking!

Knock knock!
Who's there?
Theodore.
Theodore who?
Theodore's shut!

Knock knock!
Who's there?
Isabel.
Isabel who?
Isabel not better than all this silly knocking?

Knock knock!
Who's there?
Doctor.
Doctor who?
That's right!

Knock knock!
Who's there?
Harry.
Harry who?
Harry up and open this door.

Knock knock!
Who's there?
Adolf.
Adolf who?
A dolf ball hit me on de nose!

WHOOMPF!

Knock knock!
Who's there?
Typhoo:
Typhoo who?
No, Typhoo tea!

Knock knock!
Who's there?
Dummy.
Dummy who?
Dummy a favour and open this door!

Knock knock!
Who's there?
Andy.
Andy who?
Andy man around the house!

L

LABRADOR

> **FASCINATING FACT:** If you cross a
> **labrador** with a tortoise, do you get an
> animal that goes to the newsagent's and
> comes back with last week's paper!

LADDER

DID YOU KNOW THAT POOR MAJOR OBSTACLE FELL OFF A SIXTY FOOT LADDER – HE WASN'T HURT THOUGH, HE WAS ONLY ON THE SECOND RUNG!

LAKE

FIRST YOKEL: I wonder if this **lake** is very deep?
SECOND YOKEL: It can't be, *it doesn't come up
very far on the ducks.*

LAMB CHOPS

LADY: Two nice **lamb chops** please: make them
lean.
BUTCHER: *Certainly, madam, which way?*

LAVATORIES

What do you call a lady with two **lavatories**?
Lou Lou!

LAVATORY BRUSH

What's the difference between a **lavatory brush**
and the mattermate?
What's the mattermate?
Nothing, get on with the answer!

LEAVES

What do you call a man who walks through
autumn **leaves**?
Russell!

LEGS

A girl was taking her little brother for a walk in
the park. 'Can I go and run along the top of
that wall?' he asked her.

'No,' said the sister.

'Go on,' insisted the little boy.

'Well, O K,' she said, 'but if you fall off and
break both your **legs**, *don't come running to me.*'

BROKEN LEGS AREN'T WHAT THEY'RE CRACKED UP TO BE!

What has fifty **legs** and can't walk?
Half a centipede!

What do you call a lady with one **leg** shorter than the other?
I lean!

LEMONADE

A man who drinks **lemonade** and sings at the same time is a 'pop' singer!

When is **lemonade** like a bandage?
When you use it for *thirst aid*!

LEOPARDS

FASCINATING FACT: Leopards who try to escape from zoos are always spotted.

LETTER

What do frogs write **letters** on?
Basildon Pond.

BUT 007 USES BASILDON BOND!

LETTERBOX

What do you call a man who comes through your **letterbox** in the morning?
Bill!

OK, BUT WHAT DO YOU CALL A LADY WHO SETS FIRE TO ALL HER BILLS?

I DON'T KNOW, TELL ME.

BERNADETTE!

OH, BURN A DEBT! VERY GOOD!

LETTUCE

Knock knock!
Who's there?
Lettuce.
Lettuce who?
Let us in, there's a good fellow!

LIBRARIAN

A frog went into a library. The **librarian**, trying to be kind, offered it all sorts of books to read. But the sulky frog didn't want any of them – it just sat there saying *'reddit, reddit, reddit'*.

LICE

TEACHER: Where do **lice** live?
BOY: Search me.
TEACHER: *No, thanks!*

LIGHTS

A policeman stopped a motorist. 'Excuse me, sir, your back **lights** aren't working.'

The driver got out of the car to look. Then he started to howl with despair, and tear his hair, and make a terrible scene.

'Hang on, sir,' said the officer. 'I haven't arrested you or anything – I was just pointing out that your back lights aren't working.'

'Never mind my back lights,' screamed the man. *'Where's my caravan!'*

LIONS

LION: You're a cheater!
CHEETAH: You're **lion**!

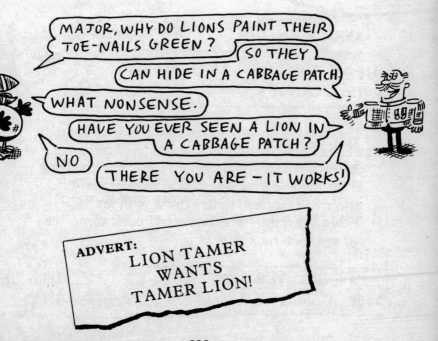

MAJOR, WHY DO LIONS PAINT THEIR TOE-NAILS GREEN?

SO THEY CAN HIDE IN A CABBAGE PATCH.

WHAT NONSENSE.

HAVE YOU EVER SEEN A LION IN A CABBAGE PATCH?

NO

THERE YOU ARE – IT WORKS!

ADVERT: LION TAMER WANTS TAMER LION!

LITTLE OLD LADY

Knock knock!
Who's there?
Little old lady.
Little old lady who?
I didn't know you could yodel!

LIVERPOOL

NEWSFLASH:
Liverpool has just signed a new player.
He insists on wearing a red cloak with
white fur hood and wellington boots. The
club says he is a Santa Forward.

LONE RANGER

HERE ARE THE FOUR BEST
LONE RANGER JOKES IN THE WORLD:

The **Lone Ranger** rushed into a pub and bought
a box of matches while Tonto carried on trotting
down the road. An old friend of his was standing
at the bar and said: 'Hey, masked stranger –
won't you stay and have a drink with me?'

'No,' said the Lone Ranger. 'I can't stop, *I've
left my injun running*!'

I THOUGHT THE LONE RANGER
DROVE AROUND IN A LONE RANGE ROVER!

What's the nearest thing to silver?
*The **Lone Ranger's** bottom.*

The **Lone Ranger** came riding over a hill on
Silver. There, on a track in front of him,
crouched Tonto, his ear to the ground.

'What are you doing, Tonto?' asked the
masked stranger.

'*Keemo Sabi* – a stage coach with six horses has
just passed this way. There were four armed men
on the top, and the front two horses were white.'

'How on earth can you tell that, Tonto?' asked
the Lone Ranger in amazement.

'*They just ran over me!*' replied his friend.

LORRY

NEWSFLASH:
A **lorry** load of glue was spilt on the M1
today – police have asked drivers to stick
to their own lanes.

A LORRY LOADED WITH HAIR RESTORER OVERTURNED. POLICE HAD TO COMB THE AREA.

LOST PROPERTY

A man with no head went into a **Lost Property** office. 'I'm sorry, sir,' said the lady behind the desk. 'You need our *Head Office!*'

LUMP

Doctor, doctor, if this **lump** on my foot gets any bigger I won't be able to get these shoes on.
Here, take this.
What is it?
The address of the nearest shoe shop.

M

MADAM
Knock knock!
Who's there?
Madam.
Madam who?
Madam finger's stuck in the keyhole!

MAGGOT
What's worse than finding a **maggot** in your apple?
Finding half a maggot in your apple!

MAGNA CARTA
TEACHER: Where was the **Magna Carta** signed?
BOY: *At the bottom!*

★ *Old* ★
Chestnut
Award

MALTESE CROSS
How do you make a **Maltese cross**?
Stamp on his foot!

MANILOW, BARRY
How do you make **Barry Manilow's** nose one metre long?
Fold it in half!

THESE JOKES ARE UNFAIR TO NOSES

MARRIAGE

BOASTFUL BOY: Do you know, Mum, when I grow up I shall **marry** any girl I please.

HIS MOTHER: What if you don't please any of them?

A rather unpleasant young man was trying hard to persuade his girl friend to **marry** him. He pointed out that his widowed father was a very rich man, and was nearly a hundred years old! The girl friend said she needed a week or two to think it over.

Two weeks later she became his step-mother!

MARTIANS

TAKE YOUR FINGER OUT OF YOUR EAR WHEN YOUR'E TALKING TO ME!

MATHS TEACHERS

What is a **maths teacher's** favourite game?

Noughts and crosses!

AT LEAST YOU HUMANS CAN ALWAYS COUNT ON YOUR FINGERS!

MAY DAY

A pilot was flying happily along when suddenly one of his engines caught fire. '**May Day**, May Day,' he shouted into his radio.

'This is the control tower,' said the voice on the radio. 'Please state your height and position.'

'*I'm about five foot eleven inches, and I'm sitting down,*' replied the pilot.

MEDICINE

A man wasn't feeling very well so he went to see the doctor. The doctor took a look at him, made some notes, and gave him a bottle of **medicine**.

'Right,' he said. 'I want you to go home and drink this medicine, followed by a nice hot bath: come back and see me next week.' The man went back a week later.

'How did you get on?' asked the doctor kindly.

'Well,' said the man. '*I managed to take the medicine, but I didn't manage to drink all the bath . . .*'

MEEK

The **meek** rule – if that's all right with everyone else.

MEMORY

Doctor, doctor, I've lost my **memory**.
When did it happen?
When did what happen?

BOY (to teacher): I've got a very good **memory**, Miss; in fact I've got a photographic mind!
TEACHER (to boy): *It's a pity it hasn't been developed . . .*

MILK

Will you join me in a glass of **milk**?
OK, you get in first.

MILLIONAIRE

RICH MAN: My wife has turned me into a **millionaire**.
HIS FRIEND: Really?
RICH MAN: *Yes, before I met her I was a multi-millionaire!*

MIND

A little girl went to her mother and said: 'Mummy, I've changed my **mind**.'
'Does the new one work any better?' replied her mother.

DO YOU HAVE DIFFICULTY MAKING UP YOUR MIND, MAJOR?

WELL . . . YES AND NO.

MINI

What time is it when an elephant sits on your **Mini**?
Time to get a new Mini!

HOW MANY ELEPHANTS CAN YOU GET IN A MINI? FOUR — TWO IN THE FRONT AND TWO IN THE BACK!

HANG ON — WHAT ABOUT ONE IN THE GLOVE COMPARTMENT?

MIRROR

A little girl's mother went into her daughter's bedroom and found her standing in front of a **mirror** with her eyes closed.

'Whatever are you doing, dear?' she asked.

'I'm trying to see what I look like when I'm asleep!' said the girl.

MOLESKIN

TEACHER: What were **moleskins** used for?
CHEEKY GIRL: *Holding moles together!*

MONEY

'I wish I had enough **money** to buy Dad a really expensive birthday present,' said Mary.

'Do you, dear, that's very kind of you,' commented her mother. 'What would you get him?'

'Oh, nothing – *I just wish I had enough money to!*'

If you tear five pound notes in half, will you double your **money**?

A doctor asked a nurse how the boy who had swallowed some **money** was getting on.

'*No change yet*,' said the nurse!

> **FASCINATING FACT: Money** doesn't grow on trees, though banks have many branches.

MONK

Is a **monk** who works in a monastery kitchen called a chip monk?

MAYBE HE'S A FISH FRIAR.

MONKEY

What **monkey** looks like a flower?
A chimp-pansy.

MONSTERS

What do sea **monsters** like to eat?
Fish and ships!

MOON

Have you heard about the two men who opened up a restaurant on the **moon**?
The food was very good, *but the place lacked atmosphere*!

MOSES

How do we know that **Moses** wore a wig?
Sometimes he was seen with Aaron, and sometimes not!

OH, I GET IT – 'HAIR ON'!

MOSQUITO

Knock knock!
Who's there?
Amos.
Amos who?
*A **mosquito** just bit me!*

Knock knock!
Who's there?
Ann.
Ann who?
*Another **mosquito** bit me as well!*

MOTHBALLS

A man went into a chemist's shop and asked to see the manager.

'These **mothballs** you sold me are no good!' he said.

'Why ever not?' asked the chemist.

'Well,' replied the man, '*I've had them for three weeks and I haven't managed to hit one moth yet!*'

MOTHERS

'My **mother** says that when she was much younger she had the most extraordinary experience. She came across a hideous, sub-human monster, a horrific alien.'

'Did she tell the police?'

'*No, she married it.*'

FIRST BOY: My **mother** does bird impressions.
SECOND BOY: Really?
FIRST BOY: *Yes, she watches me like a hawk!*

Is a very small **mother** called a *minimum*?

MOTORBIKE

Did you hear about the boy who thought that his dad had a magic **motorbike**? He'd heard his mother saying that she'd heard it turning into their drive!

MOUSE

How do you help a drowning **mouse**?
Give it mouse to mouse resuscitation!

Why can't you get milk from a **mouse**?
You can't get a bucket under a mouse!

PULL THE UDDER ONE !

FASCINATING FACT: The largest **mouse** in the world is a hippopotomouse.

MOUSETRAP

Spell **mousetrap** using only three letters.
CAT

'I'd like a **mousetrap**, and please hurry up, I've got a bus to catch.'
'Sorry, madam. *We haven't got any that big.*'

MOUTH ORGAN

A man rushed into a doctor's surgery. 'Quick doctor!' he said. 'I've swallowed a **mouth organ**!'

'You lucky chap!' said the doctor with a smile.

'Lucky! What do you mean "lucky"?' said the man.

'Well,' replied the doctor, *'what if you'd been playing a grand piano?'*

CATS LIKE TO PLAY MOUSE ORGANS !

MUSICAL

What is the most **musical** fish?
A piano tuna!

MUSKETEERS – THE THREE

Must get here,
Must get here,
Must get here.

MUTTON

Mary had a little lamb
It really was a glutton,
It quickly grew into a sheep
And ended up as **mutton**!

MYTH

TEACHER: What's a **myth**?
GIRL: *An un-married female moth!*

N

NAILS

Two men were standing on scaffolding, knocking **nails** into the walls of a house. One of the men kept tossing nails over his shoulder on to the ground. 'Why do you keep throwing nails away?' asked the other.

'They've got points at the wrong end,' said the man.

'Don't be an idiot!' scolded his mate. '*We can use them on the other side of the house!*'

MAJOR, WHERE DO YOU FILE YOUR NAILS?

I DON'T FILE THEM – I JUST CUT THEM AND THROW THEM AWAY!

NEEDLEWORK

SMALL GIRL: Our **needlework** teacher is a *so and so*.

NEPHEWS

A woman was standing on her doorstep in floods of tears.

'Whatever is the matter, dear?' asked a kind neighbour.

'Oh, it's terrible: I've just had a letter from my sister about Nigel, my favourite **nephew**. He's growing up deformed!'

'What do you mean?'

'Well, his mother says in her letter that "*Nigel has grown another foot*"!'

NET

A **net** is just a lot of holes tied together with string.

NEWSPAPER

What's in the **newspaper** on Friday nights?
Fish and chips!

> I'VE READ SO MANY NEWSPAPER REPORTS ABOUT THE DANGERS OF SMOKING CIGARETTES THAT I'VE GIVEN UP.
>
> GIVEN UP WHAT?
>
> GIVEN UP READING NEWSPAPERS OF COURSE!

NICKELBY, NICHOLAS

TEACHER: Who wrote **Nicholas Nickelby**?
SMALL BOY: *How the Dickens should I know . . .*

NOAH

Knock knock!
Who's there?
Noah.
Noah who?
Noah any more knock knock jokes?

NOSE

If your **nose** goes on strike, should you picket?

What do you call a man who gets up your **nose?**
Vic!

◁▭ see page 109 for Barry Manilow nose joke

NOTICE

A man walked into a police station and told the officer that he had lost his dog.

'Have you tried putting a **notice** in your local shops, sir?' asked the policeman.

'That wouldn't do any good,' replied the man. *'My dog can't read!'*

NOUGAT

A lady was sitting on a park bench with a bar of **nougat** sticking in each ear. A nice man came up to her and said: 'Excuse me, but you've got a bar of nougat stuck in each ear.'

She replied: 'I can't hear you, *I've got a bar of nougat stuck in each ear . . .'*

NUMBER–WRONG

A man made a telephone call.

'Hallo,' he said. 'Is that 3764?'

'No,' said the voice on the other end. 'You must have a **wrong number**.'

'*If it's a wrong number, why did you answer the phone?*' said the man.

An absent-minded professor's phone rang in the middle of the night.

'Hallo,' he said. 'Professor Nutter's phone.'

'I'm sorry,' said a voice on the phone. 'I must have a **wrong number**.'

'That's all right,' said the professor. '*I had to get up anyway to answer the phone.*'

NURSE

DOCTOR: Have you taken this patient's pulse, **Nurse**?

NURSE: No, *is it missing*?

Why did the **nurse** tiptoe past the medicine cabinet?

She didn't want to wake the sleeping pills!

O

OCTOPUS

I SAW TWO OCTOPUS LOVERS GOING DOWN THE ROAD THE OTHER DAY, MAJOR.

HOW DO YOU KNOW THEY WERE LOVERS?

THEY WERE WALKING ARM IN ARM IN ARM!

What do you get if you cross an **octopus** with a skunk?

An octopong!

NEVER ATTACK AN OCTOPUS – THEY'RE ALWAYS WELL ARMED

OFF!

MAN IN PUB: Well, I'm **off**.

ANOTHER DRINKER: *I wondered what the smell was . . .*

OINTMENT

Doctor, doctor, I've been stung by a wasp!

I'll give you some **ointment** for it.

Don't be silly – *it'll be miles away by now*!

OLD

A very **old** man was celebrating his birthday at an Old People's Home. A young interviewer from the local paper came to ask him questions: 'How do you account for the fact that you've lived so long?' she asked.

'*I reckon it's because I was born such a long time ago,*' said the man.

OLDEN DAYS

BOY: I wished I'd lived in the **olden days**, Mum.
MOTHER: Why?
BOY: *I wouldn't have to do history lessons!*

ONE-WAY STREET

POLICEMAN: Excuse me, sir, are you aware that this is a **one-way street**?
MAN: But officer – *I was only going one way*!

ONIONS

FIRST MAN: A terrible thing happened to me when I was a bit younger. My wife went out to get a pound of **onions** from the local shop, and she never came back.
SECOND MAN: How awful! Whatever did you do?
FIRST MAN: *We had carrots instead.*

OPTICIAN

Man in **optician**'s: Will I be able to read OK when I've got my new glasses?
OPTICIAN: Certainly.
MAN: Oh, good – *because I've never been able to!*

SHORT-SIGHTED FROGS GO TO HOPTICIANS!

A beautiful lady went up to a very ugly man and said: 'Excuse me, handsome, could you direct me to the **optician**'s?'

ORANGE

What's **orange** and sounds like a parrot?
A carrot!!

Why did the **orange** sit down in the middle of the road?
It wanted to play a game of squash with the cars!

I EXPECT THEY SOON RAN OUT OF JUICE !

What did the baby chicken say when its mother laid an **orange**?
'Look what mama laid!'

I GET IT — MARMALADE.

OWLS

How can you tell that **owls** are wiser than chickens?
Have you ever seen a Kentucky Fried Owl?

MUNCH CHOMP

Did you hear about the man who crossed an **owl** with a skunk?
He got a bird that smelled terrible but didn't give a hoot!

Why did the **owl** 'owl?
Because the woodpecker would peck 'er!

OYSTERS

A rich man went into a jeweller's shop. 'I'd like a really expensive present for my girl friend, please,' he said.

'This alligator tooth necklace is very expensive,' said the man behind the counter.

'What – more expensive than a pearl one?!' asked the rich man, surprised.

'Of course!' said the assistant. '*Any sissy can open an* **oyster**!'

P

PANCAKE

'Waiter, I'm in a hurry, will my **pancake** be long?'
'No, sir. *It'll be round and flat.*'

PANDA

What do you get if you cross a **panda** with a
harmonium?
Pandamonium!

PANDA CAR

A policeman who drove a **panda car** went to
see his mother. He rang the door bell. 'Who is
it?' called his mum.
   '*It's meema meema meema,*' said the panda car
driver.

PANTOMIME

GIRL: We're going to the zoo to see a **pantomime**.
BOY: The zoo? What's the pantomine called?
GIRL: *Cinderelephant!*

PAPER SHOP

A man was looking very down in the dumps.
'What's the matter, Jack?' asked a friend.
   'It's terrible,' replied Jack. 'I've just lost all
my life's savings.'
   'How did it happen?'
   'Well,' said Jack sadly, 'I bought a **paper
shop**, and *it blew away* . . .'

PARCELS

A man was in a bus with **parcels** under one arm and his other hand holding on to the rail above his head.

'Fares, please,' said the conductor.

'Oh dear,' said the man, *'would you mind holding on to this rail while I reach for my wallet?'*

PARIS

> **FASCINATING FACT:** The food is delicious in **Paris**, *especially the Trifle Tower.*

BUT IF YOU SWIM IN THE RIVER THERE YOU'LL BE IN SEINE.

OH, I SEE... INSANE!

PARK

Where do you **park** a spaceship?
At a parking meteor.

PARROT

TEACHER: If you had a **parrot**, Mary, what would you feed it on?
MARY: *Pollyfiller, Miss!*

What do you get if you cross a **parrot** with an elephant?
An animal that tells you everything it remembers.

Where do **parrots** learn to talk?
At the polytechnic.

THERE WERE A LOT OF PARROTS IN MY REGIMENT IN THE ARMY.

YES, WE WERE PARROT-TROOPERS!

REALLY?

HOW LONG WERE YOU IN THE ARMY, MAJOR?

ABOUT FIVE FOOT ELEVEN INCHES!

What do you get if you cross a **parrot** with a bee?
An animal that's always telling you how busy it is!

PARSNIPS

What do you call a man with a **parsnip** stuck in each ear?
Anything – he can't hear you!

PATIENT

Doctor, doctor, I think I'm shrinking!
Well, you'll just have to be a *little* **patient**.

PECK

What goes **peck** bang **peck** bang **peck**?
Chickens in a minefield!

129

PEDESTRIAN

A **pedestrian** was trying to cross a very busy main road. A policeman came up to him. 'There's a zebra crossing just up the road, sir,' he said.

'Well,' said the man, '*I hope he's having better luck than I am!*'

PEKING

What is a robbery called in **Peking**?
A Chinese takeaway!

PELICAN

FASCINATING FACT: It's very expensive to keep **pelicans**, you could face some very large bills.

PETALS

FIRST BOY: My new girl friend has got lips like **petals**.
SECOND BOY: Really?
FIRST BOY: Yes, *bicycle petals*!

PHONE

BILLY IS TOO ILL TO COME TO SCHOOL TODAY.

WHO IS THAT SPEAKING?

MY DAD!

PIANO

What do you call a girl with a **piano** on her head?
Joanna!

INCIDENTALLY, MAJOR OBSTACLE, DO YOU KNOW WHY PIANOS ARE SO DIFFICULT TO OPEN?

NO, WHY?

WELL, THEY'VE GOT DOZENS OF KEYS, AND THEY'RE ALL ON THE INSIDE.

PICK YOUR OWN

ADVERT:
PICK YOUR OWN FRUIT
YOU'RE NOT PICKING OURS!

PIGEONS

NEWSFLASH:
A small boy was thrown out of the zoo today for feeding the **pigeons**. He was feeding them to the lions!

PIGEONS – HOMING

What do you get if you cross a parrot with a
homing pigeon?
A bird that asks the way home!

PIGLETS

Why don't **piglets** listen to their fathers?
Because they are *boars*!

PIGS

What do you give a sick **pig**?
Oinkment!

What do you get if you cross a **pig** with itching powder?
Pork scratchings!

What plants do you use to catch **pigs** with?
Hambushes!

PIGS TAKE THEIR FOOD FOR GRUNTED!

PILLS

What **pills** do you give to an elephant that can't sleep?
Trunkquillizers!

PINK

What's **pink** with a curly tail and drinks blood?
A hampire!

PIRANHA FISH

What's the difference between a **piranha fish** and a raspberry milk shake?
A raspberry milk shake doesn't bite you to death!

PLANK

What do you call a man with a **plank** on his head?
Edward!
What do you call a man with *three* **planks** on his head?
Edward wood wood!

PLUM

What do you get if you cross a **plum** with a lion?
A purple people eater!

POCKET CALCULATOR

A boy looked as if he was having difficulty with a maths test, so his helpful teacher came over to him and said: 'If you like you can use a **pocket calculator**.'

'No thanks, Miss,' said the boy, '*I already know how many pockets I've got.*'

INCIDENTALLY, MAJOR OBSTACLE, WHAT'S THE FASTEST WAY TO COUNT COWS?

I DON'T KNOW.

USE A COWCULATOR!

WELL DON'T GET TOO CLOSE OR YOU'LL GET A PAT ON THE HEAD!

POCKETS

MATHS TEACHER: Michael, if you had six pounds in one **pocket**, and seven pounds in another pocket, and three pounds in your back pocket, what would you have?
MICHAEL: *Someone else's trousers on!*

POLAR BEARS

What do **polar bears** have for lunch?
Iceburgers!

POLICE

Knock knock!
Who's there?
Police.
Police who?
Police hurry up and open this door, we're freezing out here!

POLICEMAN

A **policeman** saw a tortoise walking up the M1. He screeched up to it in his police car.
'What do you think you're doing on the motorway?' he asked the poor animal.
'*About two metres an hour,*' said the tortoise.

A **policeman** lived at:
999, Letsby Avenue

What did the three-headed **policeman** say?
'*Hello, Hello, Hello!*'

What is a **policeman's** favourite food?
Truncheon meat sandwiches!

POLICE STATION
A man went up to another man in the street and said: 'Excuse me, sir, could you direct me to the nearest **police station**?

'I'm sorry, I don't know where it is,' the other replied.

'*Oh, good*,' said the first man. '*Stick 'em up!*'

POLYGON
TEACHER: What's a **polygon**?
GIRL: *An empty parrot cage, Miss!*

PORCUPINE
What did the baby **porcupine** say to the cactus?
Hello, Mum!

POSTMAN PAT
What do you call **Postman Pat** when he retires?
PAT!

POTFER
A man went fishing. When he got home his wife asked him what he had caught.

'Three trout and a **potfer**.'

'What's a potfer?' asked his wife.

'*Cooking the trout in*,' said the man.

PRAYER
MOTHER: Have you said your **prayers** tonight?
GIRL: Yes, I prayed that God would make four and four make nine.
MOTHER: Why?
GIRL: *Because that's what I put in my maths test.*

PRICKLY
What's green and **prickly**?
A seasick hedgehog!

PRICKLY PEAR
TEACHER: What's a **prickly pear**?
BOY: *Two hedgehogs!*

▭ **see more Hedgehog jokes on page 82**

PRISON
MAN: My best friend has just been sent to
prison because of his beliefs.
HIS WIFE: That's terrible! But what do you
mean?
MAN: Well, *he believed that the night watchman
was asleep!*

PRUNES
Two **prunes** were arrested for being stewed.
They were remanded in custardy.

Why did the **prune** go out with a fig?
He couldn't get a date.

Police report that someone has stolen a lorry-load
of **prunes**.
They are looking for a man on the run.

PSYCHOLOGIST
Doctor, doctor, I keep seeing green hairy
monsters with hideous faces!
Have you seen a **psychologist**?
No, *just green hairy monsters with hideous faces!*

PUBS

What do you call a lady who goes into a **pub** and starts to juggle with the drinks?
Beatrix!

> OH, I SEE, YOU MEAN BEER TRICKS!

> VERY GOOD, MAJOR OBSTACLE — BUT WHAT DO YOU CALL HER IF SHE THEN STARTS TO PLAY SNOOKER AS WELL?

> BEATRIX POTTER OF COURSE!!

> HURRAY!

PUFFINS

Why don't elephants like **puffins**?
They can't turn the pages over very easily!

PUPPETEERS

> **FASCINATING FACT: Puppeteers** get work by pulling strings.

PUPPY

A small boy asked his mother if he could have a **puppy** for Christmas.
'No,' she replied. '*You'll have turkey like everybody else.*'

What did Sting sing to his new **puppy**?
'*Every mess you make!*'

PURPLE

WHAT'S PURPLE, WITH YELLOW SPOTS AND HAIRY LEGS AND A POISONOUS STING AND GREAT BIG FEELERS?

I DON'T KNOW.

NEITHER DO I BUT ONE'S JUST GONE DOWN YOUR NECK!

PUTTY

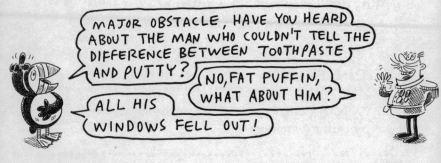

MAJOR OBSTACLE, HAVE YOU HEARD ABOUT THE MAN WHO COULDN'T TELL THE DIFFERENCE BETWEEN TOOTHPASTE AND PUTTY?

NO, FAT PUFFIN, WHAT ABOUT HIM?

ALL HIS WINDOWS FELL OUT!

PYJAMAS

BOASTFUL MAN: When I was big game hunting once, I shot a tiger in my **pyjamas**.
BORED LADY: *What was a tiger doing wearing your pyjamas?*

Q

ALTHOUGH Q IS RATHER A SILLY LETTER — ALWAYS NEEDING A U TO HOLD HANDS WITH — IT IS DEFINITELY NOT FUNNY. THE WORDS BEGINNING WITH A Q ARE THINGS LIKE OUR DEAR QUEEN, QUADRAGESIMA, QUADRAPHONIC, QUINQUAGESIMA AND QUOD. SO IT'S NO SURPRISE THAT THERE ARE NO JOKES BEGINNING WITH THE LETTER Q! IF YOU KNOW ANY — WRITE THEM IN YOURSELF!

R

RABBIT

WHAT DO YOU CALL A MAN WITH A RABBIT UP HIS JUMPER?

WARREN!

What do you get if you
pour boiling water down a **rabbit** hole?
Hot, cross bunnies!

RADIO

WHY ARE YOU BURYING THAT RADIO, SON?

THE BATTERIES ARE DEAD!

RAT POISON

A man was having trouble with rats so he went into a shop and asked the man behind the counter if he sold **rat poison**.

'No,' said the man. 'Have you tried Boots?'

'Look, I want to poison them, not kick them to death . . .' said the man indignantly.

RED

What's **red** and rather stupid?
A blood clot.

RED ISN'T AS FUNNY AS YELLOW OR GREEN!

RELATIONSHIP

A boy was talking to his mother. 'I think my new girl friend and I have a love-hate **relationship**,' he said.

'What do you mean, dear?' asked his mother.
'Well, I love her, and she hates me!'

REPTILES

What **reptiles** are good at arithmetic?
Adders!

REQUESTS

A man was having a meal in a very posh hotel.
'Waiter,' he said. 'Does the band do **requests**?'
'Yes, sir.'
'Good – *ask them to go and play outside!*'

RESTAURANTS

A **restaurant** claimed to cook anything a customer wanted, so some clever dick went in and sat down and asked for a rhinoceros omelette and chips. 'Certainly, sir,' said the waiter and he went off to the kitchen. A few minutes later he returned and whispered to the clever dick, *'I'm sorry, sir, we seem to have run out of potatoes.'*

MAN IN RESTAURANT: How long have you worked here?
WAITRESS: Two months.
MAN: *Oh, well it can't have been you who took my order . . .*

ADVERT:
EAT AT YUCKO'S FAMOUS
TAKE AWAY RESTAURANT!
COME IN,
SIT DOWN,
EAT A MEAL
AND TAKE IT AWAY
WHEN YOU LEAVE!

A man in a **restaurant** had finished his meal but wasn't very pleased with it. 'What's wrong?' asked the waiter.

'Well, my chop was very hard and tough.'

'That's probably because it was a karate chop, sir,' said the waiter.

A lion went into a **restaurant** and sat down.
The waiter went over to it: 'What would you
like to eat, sir?' he asked.

'*You,*' *said the lion, licking his lips!*

RHINOCEROS

A **rhinoceros** went into a pub and sat down
on a bar stool. 'I'd like a pint of beer please,
landlord,' it asked politely.

'Right!' thought the landlord. 'Here's a chance
to make some money.' He poured out the beer
and handed it to the rhinoceros:

'That's five pounds, please.'

The rhinoceros paid the money and started
to drink the beer. The landlord thought he'd
better make conversation with his new customer.
'We don't get many rhinoceroses in here,' he said.

'*I'm not surprised, with beer at five pounds a
pint!*' said the rhinoceros.

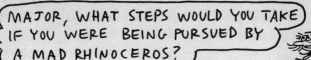

MAJOR, WHAT STEPS WOULD YOU TAKE IF YOU WERE BEING PURSUED BY A MAD RHINOCEROS?

VERY BIG ONES!

RIVER

What do you call a girl who stands with one leg on each side of a **river**?
Bridget!

And what do you call a man who swims in slow circles in a **river**?
Eddy!

ROAD

Why did the chicken cross the **road**?
To get to the other side.

Old *
Chestnut
Award

Why did the hedgehog cross the **road**?
To see his flat mate!

Why *didn't* the skeleton **cross the road**?
He didn't have the guts!

Why did the cockerel cross the **road**?
To show that he wasn't chicken.

Why did the man with one arm cross the **road**?
To get to the second-hand shop!

Why did the Manx cat cross the **road**?
To get to a re-tail shop!

Why did the dinosaur cross the **road**?
There weren't any chickens in those days!

Why did the elephant cross the **road**?
It was the chicken's day off!

INCIDENTALLY, WHAT DO YOU GET IF YOU CROSS THE M1 WITH A SKATEBOARD?

RUNOVER!

ROBBER

FIRST MAN: Did you hear about the **robber** who went into a bank and was arrested?
SECOND MAN: No.
FIRST MAN: *It was full of coppers!*

What do you call two **robbers**?
A pair of nickers!

NEWSFLASH:
A **robber** has been sentenced for stealing a calendar. He got twelve months.

ROBIN

Knock knock!
Who's there?
Robin.
Robin who?
Robin you, hand over your money!

ROCK CAKES

If someone offers you a **rock cake**, take your pick.

CLIMBERS LIKE ROCK CAKES!

ROLLERS

Why do women go to bed at night with **rollers** in their hair?
So they can *wake up curly in the morning*.

ROLL, SAUSAGE

How do you make a **sausage roll**?
Push it down a hill.

ROLL, SWISS

How do you make a **Swiss roll**?
Push him off a cliff!

ROLLS-ROYCE

A man set his heart on buying a **Rolls-Royce**. For years and years he saved every penny he could, until finally he had enough money to buy one. He went to the car showroom and selected the one he wanted. When the salesman asked for the money – a gigantic sum – the man turned out his pockets and put all his money on the car salesman's desk. The salesman counted it. 'I'm sorry, sir,' he said. 'But you're four pence short of the price.'

   'Don't worry,' said the excited buyer, and he rushed out into the street and went up to a newspaper seller. 'Excuse me, mate,' he said.

'Could you spare me four pence? I want to buy a Rolls-Royce.'

'*That's OK,*' said the newspaper seller. '*Here's eight pence – get one for me too!*'

ROOM

What's the smallest **room** in a house?
A mushroom!

ROSE

What do you get if you cross a **rose** with a black mamba?
I don't know, but don't smell it!

RUDE

Who said 'get stuffed' to the big bad wolf?
*Little **Rude** Riding Hood!*

RULE

100 cm pieces of plastic **Rule** OK?

RUN-DOWN

ADVERT: AVOID FEELING RUN-DOWN LOOK BOTH WAYS BEFORE CROSSING THE ROAD!

S

SAFARI

TEACHER: John, do Eskimos go on **safari**?
JOHN: *Not safaris I know!*

SAMSON

Samson was a great entertainer. He brought the house down!

SANTA CLAUS

A doctor has reported that several small children are afraid of **Santa Claus** coming down their chimney. He says they may be suffering from *Santaclaustrophobia*.

SANTA CLAUS'S WIFE

What do you call **Mrs Santa Claus**?
Mary Christmas, of course!

SAUSAGES

Sausage Rolls – OK

Sausages are rude – they spit.

SCHOOL

What did Santa Claus learn at **school**?
How to pass his Ho, Ho levels!

SCHOOL SWOT

My lad must be the **school swot** – the other kids pick him up and bash flies with him!

SCOTLAND

What lives in **Scotland** and never wins the football pools?
The Luckless Monster!

SCOTLAND YARD

NEWSFLASH: All the lavatory seats have been stolen from **Scotland Yard.** Police say they have nothing to go on.

SEA

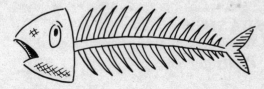

What lies at the bottom of the **sea** and shakes?
A nervous wreck!

> **FASCINATING FACT**: When Moses
> parted the Red **Sea** he did it using a
> *Sea-Saw*.

SEAGULL

A man went into a doctor's surgery with a large
white **seagull** on the top of his head.
'What seems to be the trouble?' asked the
doctor.
'*Well*,' said the seagull, '*I've got this man stuck to
my feet!*'

What do you call a man with a **seagull** on his
head?
Cliff!

Two not very bright gentlemen were walking along the beach.

'Look,' said one of them suddenly. 'A dead **seagull**!'

'Where?' said his friend, looking up in the sky.

SEASICK

What do you give a **seasick** gorilla?
Plenty of room!

SECONDS

How many **seconds** in one year?
Only twelve, *the second of each month*!

SHAKESPEARE

TEACHER: What did **Shakespeare** use to write with?
BOY: *A pencil – either a 2B or not 2B.*

SHARKS

Why is it easy to fool a **shark**?
They'll swallow anything!

BOY: Have you ever seen a man-eating **shark**?
HIS FRIEND: *No, but I've seen a man eating turkey – my dad at Christmas!*

★ Old ★ Chestnut Award

SHEEP

What do you call a **sheep** with a machine-gun?
Lambo!

> **FASCINATING FACT:** Friendly **sheep** are
> called *pen friends*.

DO SHEEP GET SHEARED AT A
BAA BAA'S SHOP?

YES, BUT THEY GO SHOPPING
AT WOOLWORTHS.

NEWSFLASH:
A man was fined for excessive cruelty today.
He went into a field full of **sheep** and lambs
and shouted, '*mint sauce!*'

What do you get if you cross a **sheep** with a
leopard and a kangaroo?
A spotted woolly jumper!

What do you get if you cross a **sheep** with a
penguin and a kangaroo?
A black and white woolly jumper!

Did little Bo Peep lose her **sheep** because she had a crook with her?

SHEEP DOGS

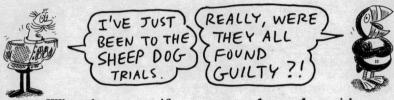

I'VE JUST BEEN TO THE SHEEP DOG TRIALS.

REALLY, WERE THEY ALL FOUND GUILTY?!

What do you get if you cross a **sheep dog** with a daisy?
A collieflower!

SHIP

What **ship** can't you sink?
Friendship!

AAAhhhhhh!

SHOPPING

Where does a really scruffy person go **shopping**?
Shabbytat!

SHOW JUMPING

SMALL GIRL IN RIDING GEAR: When I took my pony **show jumping** we lost by a single refusal.
IMPRESSED ADULT: Really?
GIRL: *Yes, he refused to get out of the horse box!*

SICK SQUID

A man went up to a friend of his and gave him a large squid.
'*Here's the* **sick squid** I owe you,' he said.

SKELETON

There was once a **skeleton** who was Emperor of France. His name was Napoleon Bones-Apart.

IF NAPOLEON HAD BEEN HIT BY A CANNON BALL, HE WOULD HAVE BEEN NAPOLEON BLOWN-APART!

If a **skeleton** pushes your door bell, is he a dead ringer?

Why didn't the **skeleton** go to the disco?
He didn't have any body to go with!

WOT – NO GHOUL-FRIEND?

SKIRTING BOARD

What do you get if you cross an elephant with a mouse?
*Big holes in your **skirting boards**!*

SKUNK

How many **skunks** do you need to make a smell?
Just a phewww!!

SLATES

What do you call a girl with **slates** on her head?
Roof.

OH, YOU MEAN RUTH !

SLUG

MAN IN RESTAURANT: Waiter, there's a **slug** in my salad.
WAITER: I'm sorry, sir, *I didn't know you're a vegetarian*!

SMELL

How do you stop a dead fish from **smelling**?
Hold its nose!

ADVERT: PONGO!
A DEODORANT COMBINED WITH VANISHING CREAM THE DEODORANT DOESN'T WORK VERY WELL BUT IF YOU SPRAY IT ON EVERYONE WONDERS WHERE THE SMELL IS COMING FROM!

SMOKED HADDOCK

HAVE YOU SMOKED HADDOCK, WAITER?

MENU

NO, SIR, I COULDN'T GET IT TO LIGHT.

SNAILS

TEACHER: Where do you find giant **snails**?
GIRL: On a *giant's fingers and toes*!

SNAKE

A daddy **snake** and his little son snake were wiggling down the road. 'Dad,' said the little snake suddenly. 'Are we the sort of snake that crushes people to a hideous death, or are we the sort that poisons them with our deadly venom?'

'We crush them to a hideous death, son. Why?'

'*I'm so glad,*' said the little snake. '*I just bit my lip!*'

What do you call a very polite **snake**?
A civil serpent!

SNOB

Mr Toff was such a **snob** that he made his kids eat their candy floss with a knife and fork!

I EXPECT HE WORE A TIE WITH HIS PYJAMAS !!

SNOOKER

Doctor, doctor, I think I'm turning into a
snooker ball.
Well wait at the end of the cue then.

SNOOPY

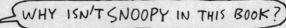

WHY ISN'T SNOOPY IN THIS BOOK?

HE DOESN'T WORK FOR PEANUTS!

SNORE

A man went to the doctor: 'It's terrible doctor – I
snore so loudly that I wake myself up!'
   'Well, why don't you sleep in another room?'
asked the doctor.

SOAPFLAKES

DID YOU HEAR ABOUT THE GIRL WHO
GAVE HER DAD SOAPFLAKES
INSTEAD OF CORNFLAKES FOR
BREAKFAST?   WAS HE CROSS?

WELL HE CERTAINLY
FOAMED AT THE MOUTH!

SOLDIERS

What are baby **soldiers** called?
Infant-ry!

SOUP

'Waiter!' shouted an angry man in a restaurant.
'This **soup** isn't fit for a pig!'
   'I'm sorry, sir; *I'll fetch you some that is!*'

'Waiter! This **soup** is the end!'
'I know, sir. *It's oxtail!*'

see lots of Fly in soup jokes on page 65

SPADE

What do you call a man with a **spade** on his head?
Doug!

What do you call a man *without* a **spade** on his head?
Dougless!

SPAIN

Spain Rules – Olé!

I THOUGHT 'OLÉ' WAS WHAT SPANISH FARMERS SAY TO THEIR HENS!

SPIDERS

What do you call an Irish **spider**?
Paddy long legs!

MUM, I'VE JUST SWALLOWED A SPIDER.

SHALL I GET THE DOCTOR TO GIVE YOU SOMETHING FOR IT?

NO, LET IT STARVE TO DEATH!

SPOONS

WHICH HAND DO YOU STIR YOUR TEA WITH?

NEITHER— I USE A SPOON.

Doctor, doctor, I think I've swallowed a **spoon**. *Well sit there and don't stir*.

STAIRS
Stairs are on the up and up!

STEAK
A man was sitting in a restaurant and the waiter brought his food. The man was horrified to see that the waiter had his thumb on the **steak** that he had ordered. 'Waiter!' he snapped. 'You've got your thumb on my steak!'

'I know,' said the waiter calmly. '*But you wouldn't want it to fall on the floor again, would you?*'

STEAMROLLER

NEWSFLASH:
The man who was run over in the high street today by a **steamroller** has been taken to hospital. He can be visited in wards 6, 7 and 8.

STEPS

What goes ninety-nine **steps** tap, ninety-nine
steps, tap?
A centipede with a wooden leg!

STEW

LADY IN CAFE: Waiter, is there any **stew** on
the menu?
WAITER: No, madam, *I wiped it off*!

STEW, IRISH

Knock knock!
Who's there?
Irish Stew.
Irish stew who?
Irishstew in the name of the law!

STRAW

What do you call a man with **straw** in his hair?
Rick!

OH YES, LIKE A HAYRICK!

STRIPES

What's got **stripes** and pulls a plough?
A caterpillar tractor!

SUN

LAST NIGHT I WENT TO BED
WONDERING WHERE THE SUN HAD GONE,
BUT THIS MORNING IT DAWNED ON ME!

SURGERY

HERE IS A LIST OF PEOPLE YOU MIGHT FIND IN A DOCTOR'S SURGERY:

Auntie Septic
Anna Bolic-Steroids
Eli Astoplast
Sir Jeckle Appliance
Varicose others!

ADVERT:
COME TO OUR
HILARIOUS HOSPITAL
LET OUR SURGEONS OPERATE
ON YOU
THEY'LL HAVE YOU
IN STITCHES

SUITCASE
A man went to the doctor and told him that he thought he was turning into a **suitcase**. The doctor sent him packing!

SWALLOW
What do you get if you cross a **swallow** with an elephant?
Broken telephone wires!

SWEETS
TEACHER: Jane, if you had ten **sweets** and John asked you for one, how many would you have?
JANE: *Ten!*

T

TALKING DOGS

A man went into a pub and told the barman that his dog was a **talking dog**. 'I bet you five pounds I can get him to answer any question you like to ask him,' he said.

'OK,' said the barman. 'How are you?'

'Rough!' barked the dog.

'And what do you call the top of a house?'

'Roof!' barked the dog again.

'Right,' said the barman. 'Now then, who was the manager of the English football team in the Mexico World Cup?'

'Rough!' barked the dog.

'What a load of rubbish!' said the barman. 'Give me my five pounds.'

The man gave the barman the money and started to leave the pub. On the way through the door the dog turned to the man and said,

'*I remember now. It was Alf Ramsey!!*'

TARZAN

Where does **Tarzan** buy his swimming trunks?
At a jungle sale!

What were **Tarzan**'s last words?
'*Who put grease on this vine?*'

TARZAN IS A SWINGER!

TAXI

A man and his wife were getting ready to leave a restaurant and go home. 'Waiter,' he said, 'Please would you call me a **taxi**.'

'Certainly, sir,' said the waiter. *'You're a taxi!'*

TEA

'Doctor, doctor, every time I drink a mug of **tea** I get a pain up my nose.'

'Try taking the spoon out of the mug.'

TEACHERS

Why was the **teacher** cross-eyed?
He couldn't control his pupils!

JANE: Mummy, I don't want to go to school today. Everyone there hates me, and I don't like school dinners, and the boys tease me and they all call me names and things; it's horrible!
JANE'S MOTHER: Don't be silly Jane, you must go – *you're the **teacher**!*

Teacher: I'd like to compliment you on your school work, Samantha. When are you going to do some?

Teachers are special because they are in a class of their own.

BOY: **Teacher** likes me.
HIS MOTHER: How do you know?
BOY: *She puts kisses next to my sums!*

★ Old ★
Chestnut
Award

What do you call a **teacher** when he walks into the classroom door?
Careless!

TEDDY BEARS
A **Teddy Bear**'s favourite drink is ginger bear.

How do you start a **teddy bear** race?
'Ready, Teddy, GO!'

I KNOW HOW TO START A GLOW WORM RACE, YOU SHOUT: 'READY STEADY GLOW!'

TELEPHONE
If you **telephone** 666, what do you get?
The Australian police!

What do you get if you **telephone** 68496837259783754968572?
A sore finger!

I KNOW WHAT THE BIG TELEPHONE SAID TO THE LITTLE TELEPHONE — 'YOU'RE TOO YOUNG TO BE ENGAGED!'

TELEVISION

WHAT'S ON TELEVISION TONIGHT, SON?

JUST THE GOLDFISH BOWL AS USUAL

Television is a cemetery for old films.

TENNIS

What do you call a girl who lies across the middle of a **tennis** court?
Annette!

Tennis is such a noisy game; the players are always raising a racket!

THEATRE

A man was sitting in the **theatre** when a large lady squeezed past him and went out to the lavatory. As she went past she stood on his foot.

When she came back in she whispered to him: 'Excuse me, did I just stand on your foot?'

'Yes,' said the man.

'Oh good, then this is my row,' she replied.

THUMB

LADY IN RESTAURANT: Waiter, your **thumb** is in my soup!

WAITER: Don't worry, madam, *it's not hot*!

◁▭see the Steak and Thumb joke on page 160

TICK

What goes **tick** woof, tick woof, tick woof?
A watch dog!

TIDDLEY POM

Is a **Tiddley Pom** an Englishman who goes to Australia and has too much to drink?

TIGER

An explorer felt rather nervous about going into the jungle.

'Are you sure there are no **tigers** there?' he asked the native guide.

'Certain,' said the guide. *'The lions have chased them all away!'*

TIME

How do witches know what **time** it is?
They look at their witch watches!

Why did the boy throw his alarm clock out of the window?
He wanted to see if **time** flies.

TITANIC
What do you get if you cross the North Atlantic with the **Titanic**?
About half-way!

TOADS

TOADS ARE NOT AS FUNNY AS FROGS!

What **toad** goes croak dot croak dot croak dot dot croak!
A Morse toad!

TOAST
How does a monkey make **toast**?
He puts a piece of bread under a gorilla!

TOILET
What animal do you find in a **toilet**?
A wash hand bison!

TOMATOES
A boy came to school one morning with a huge lump on his forehead. 'James,' said the teacher. 'However did you get that terrible bump on the head?'

'A **tomato** fell on it, Miss.'

'A tomato!' said the teacher in amazement. 'It must have been a mighty big tomato.'

'No, Miss,' replied James. '*It was quite small, but it was in a tin.*'

TONGUE

A small boy rushed downstairs late one night:
'Daddy, Daddy, come quickly,' he wailed.
'There's something under my bed, with it's
tongue hanging out!'

'Don't be silly, son, *that's your shoe,*' said his
father.

TONSILS

What did the **tonsils** say to each other?
Let's get dressed up, *the doctor's going to take us
out tonight.*

TORTOISE

Why did the **tortoise** cross the road?
To get to the Shell Garage!

see page 145 for more 'crossing the road' jokes!

FASCINATING FACT: If you cross a
tortoise with a cow you get long-life milk.

TOUR DE FRANCE

Did you hear about the man who won the **Tour
de France**? Straight after the race he disappeared
for three weeks. He was doing a lap of honour!

TOWER OF LONDON

What's black and shiny, off its rocker, and lives
at the **Tower of London**?
A raven loony!

TOYSHOP

A lady went into a **toyshop**: 'I'd like something for my son, please,' she said.

'Certainly, madam,' said the assistant. *'How much were you thinking of asking?'*

TRAFFIC LIGHT

What did the **traffic light** say to the car?
'Don't look now, I'm changing!'

TRAINS

What do you call a **train** full of toffee?
A chew chew train.

What do you call an underground **train** full of professors?
A tube of smarties!

Will the **train** now standing on platform ten please get back on to the rails.

Don't fall asleep near a railway – **trains** run over sleepers!

TREE

What did the beaver say to the **tree**?
'Nice to gnaw you!'

TREE SURGEON

I WANTED TO BE A TREE SURGEON, BUT I COULDN'T STAND THE SIGHT OF SAP.

TROUSERS

TEACHER TO SCRUFFY BOY: Jimmy, you've got holes in your **trousers**.
JIMMY: *Of course I have, otherwise how could I get my legs into them?*

TURNIP

Knock knock!
Who's there?
Turnip.
Turnip who?
Turnip your trousers, they're too long!

TWIT

HEY, MAJOR! HOW DO YOU KEEP A TWIT IN SUSPENSE?

I DON'T KNOW, PLEASE TELL ME ...GO ON ... TELL ME.

U, V, & W!

UDDER
What has four legs, an **udder** and flies?
A cow!

UMBRELLA
What type of **umbrella** did Napoleon use when
it rained?
A wet one!

VAMPIRES
What's a **vampire**'s favourite food?
Neck-tarines!

YES, BUT FOR BREAKFAST THEY PREFER READY NECK !

I THOUGHT THEY LIKED GRAVEY

FANGS AIN'T WHAT THEY USED TO BE.

What's a **vampire**'s favourite soup?
Scream of mushroom!

VEGETABLES

VEST

What did the policeman say to his belly button?
*You're under a **vest**!*

VICARS

Two **vicars** were walking in a garden when one of them looked carefully at the roses and saw that they had greenfly on them.
'*Let us spray,*' said the other.

A **vicar** was christening a pair of twins. He was supposed to call them Kate and Sidney. He got a bit muddled and they ended up being christened Steak and Kidney.

* Old *
Chestnut
Award

VIOLETS

VIOLIN

Did you hear about the girl who was so unmusical that it took her a year to get a sound out of a **violin**? *For the first eleven months she blew it . . .*

VIPER

Why didn't the **viper** viper nose?
'Cos the adder 'ad 'er 'andkerchief.

VIPERS EAT HISS FINGERS!

WAGES

A boy came home from the shop where he did a holiday job. 'I've got really good news, Dad,' he said. 'They've doubled my **wages**!'

'Really?' said his father, surprised.

'Yes, instead of giving me twenty pounds every week, *they are going to give me twenty pounds every two weeks*!'

WALLY!

Wally couldn't tell his two cows apart but one day he wondered if one of them might be just slightly taller than the other one. He measured them and sure enough, *the black and white one was an inch taller than the brown one*!

WARTHOG

WARTHOG: What's that ugly animal over there?
HIPPO: That's a **warthog**.
WARTHOG: *How terrible to have to go around looking like that!*

WASHING MACHINE

What do you call a nun with a **washing machine** on her head?
Sistermatic!

WASPS

Where do ill **wasps** go to get better?
Waspital!

HOW COME WASPS GET SO MUCH TIME OFF FOR PICNICS?

WATCH

A girl was showing her new **watch** to a friend in the playground.

'Look at this watch – it's amazing. My dad gave it to me, it cost ninety pence at the garage.'

'What's amazing about it?' asked the friend.

'It's amazing that it's still going!'

WATER

What do you give a man with **water** on the brain?
A tap on the head.

Have you heard about the man who gave up **water** skiing?
He couldn't find any sloping lakes.

When is **water** not water?
When it's dripping!

TEACHER: Spell **water**.
BOY: HIJKLMNO.
TEACHER: That doesn't spell water.
BOY: Yes, it does – *it's all the letters from H to O!*

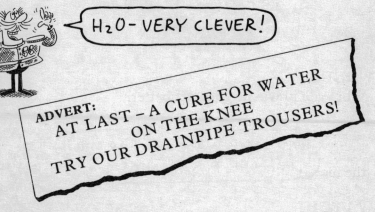

H₂O – VERY CLEVER!

WATER RATS
Where do **water rats** keep their money?
In river banks!

WEASELS

FASCINATING FACT: It's easy to tell the difference between **weasels** and stoats. Weasels are weaselly wecognized and stoats are stoatally different.

WEDDING

A small boy was at his big sister's **wedding**. When the vicar asked who was giving the bride away, he piped up, *'Why, what's she done wrong?'*

WEIGHT TRAINING

GIRL: My stupid brother does **weight training**.
HER FRIEND: Really?
GIRL: *Yes, he stands about and waits for trains!*

WELL

A man fell down a deep **well**.
'Have you broken anything?' his friend called down to him.
'No, there's nothing down here to break!' replied the man.

WETTER

What gets **wetter**
the more it dries?
A towel.

★ *Old* ★
Chestnut
Award

WHALE

How do you know the weight of a **whale**?
Take it to a whale weigh station!

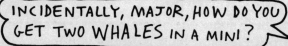

INCIDENTALLY, MAJOR, HOW DO YOU GET TWO WHALES IN A MINI?

I KNOW THAT ONE. YOU GO ACROSS THE SEVERN BRIDGE — TO WALES!

WHISPERING

ANNOUNCEMENT: Whispering is not aloud.

WILTON

What happens if you cross a **Wilton** with an elephant?
You get a huge pile on your carpet!

WIND

Doctor, doctor, I've got **wind**, can you give me something for it?
Yes, how about a kite . . .

WINDOW

A man wasn't feeling very well so he went to the doctor. 'O K,' said the doctor when he had examined him. 'I want you to turn and face the **window**, and stick your tongue out.'

'Will that cure me?' said the man.

'No,' said the doctor. 'But *I don't like the man who lives in the house opposite!*'

WINDOW SHOPPING

Did you hear about the man who went **window shopping**? He came back with five windows.

WINE GLASSES

'Mummy, I'm going to buy you a lovely set of **wine glasses** for Christmas,' said little Jason.

'That's very kind, dear, but I've already got a set of wine glasses.'

'You haven't,' said Jason sadly. '*I've just dropped them.*'

WINKERS

A man wanted to know if the indicator **winkers** on his car were working properly so he stopped his car and asked a small boy to look at them and tell him.

'Are they working?' said the man.

'YES NO YES NO YES NO YES NO,' said the boy!

WINE

What animal do we get **wine** from?
A wine-oceros!

WITCHES

Why are **witches** good at English?
They are brilliant at *spelling*!

An old **witch** thought that she would make a fortune telling fortunes, so she bought a crystal ball, *but she couldn't see any future in it*!

What **witches** do you find in the desert?
Sandwitches!

I MET TWO WITCHES WHO WERE TWINS – I JUST COULDN'T TELL WITCH WITCH WAS WHICH!

WOBBLE

What lies in a pram and **wobbles**?
A jellybaby!

What flies and **wobbles**?
A jellicopter!

WOOD

A boy was working in a carpentry lesson. 'Please, sir,' he said to the woodwork teacher, 'I need some more **wood**.'

'MORE wood!' said the teacher in amazement. *'Wood doesn't grow on trees you know!'*

WOODWORK

Did you hear about the **woodwork** teacher who broke all his teeth?
He bit his nails!

WOODWORM

FASCINATING FACT: If you cross a **woodworm** with an elephant, you get very big holes in your furniture.

Did you hear about the idiot **woodworm**?
It was found dead – *in a brick!*

WOOL – STEEL

SMALL BOY: Mum, what is **steel wool** used for?
IMPATIENT MOTHER: *Knitting wire netting with!*

WORDS

What two **words** have the most letters?
Post Office.

WORDS – RUDE

A boy showed his school report to his father and
then took it to his mother. 'What did your dad
say when he'd read it?' she asked.
 'Can I use **rude words**?'
 'No, of course not.'
 '*He didn't say anything then,*' said the boy.

WORMS

DID YOU HEAR ABOUT THE LITTLE
BOY WHO DID BIRD IMPRESSIONS?
HE ATE WORMS!

FASCINATING FACT: If you want to know
which end of a **worm** is the head, conduct
the following experiment: put a worm in a
saucer of flour, blow some pepper over it.
Watch the flour to see which end sneezes!

WRINKLED

What's green, three metres tall and **wrinkled**,
and likes knitting?
Incredible Hulk's granny!

see page 55 for wrinkled elephant joke!

X-rated jokes

What's green and
hangs from trees?
Giraffe snot!

What noise does a dog make if you set fire to it?
WOOOOOFFFFFF!

What noise does a cat make if you throw it out
of a skyscraper?
MEEEOOOOOOOWWWWW!!

OLD MOTTO: A bird in the hand makes it
difficult to pick your nose.

A man was standing on a street corner selling
small tortoises from a tray. A man who had
obviously had rather too much to drink came
swaying up to him and bought one.
   A few minutes later the drunk returned. 'I'd
like another of your little brown pies please,' he
said. '*I'd like one with not such a hard crust.*'

Why was the beach wet?
Because the seaweed.

Definition of a sadist: someone who would put a drawing pin on the electric chair!

'Mummy, Mummy, I don't want to go to America.'
'Be quiet, Henry, and keep swimming.'

TEACHER: What is a cannibal?
BOY: I don't know, Miss.
TEACHER: Well what would you be if you ate your parents?
BOY: *An orphan, Miss.*

Man in a restaurant who has spilt his soup down his trousers:
'Waiter! I've got soup in my flies!'

Did you hear about the dentist who became a brain surgeon?
His drill slipped!

Ding, dong, bell,
Pussy's in the well.
We put some disinfectant down
And that has cured the smell!

What does a girl do sitting down, that a boy does standing up and a dog does on three legs?
Shakes hands!

'I washed my cat last night, and it died.'
    'That's odd, I can't see how washing a cat could do it any harm.'
    '*I think it may have been the spin drying that did it!*'

The French think the English are rotten cooks –
they even burnt Joan of Arc!

What's yellow and smells of bananas?
Monkey sick!

Where do you find a dog with no legs?
The last place you put it!

'Doctor, doctor! I can't feel my legs!'
'I'm not surprised – *I've just cut your arms off!*'

Someone in class made a rude noise. 'Stop that!'
said the teacher.
    'OK,' said one of his pupils. '*Which way did
it go?*'

What's the difference between a letterbox and
a cow's bottom?
I don't know.
*Well I wouldn't ask you to post a letter for me
then!*

What do you call an Irishman who's been dead
for five hundred years?
Peat!

NEWSFLASH:
Someone has cut a hole in the fence of the
nudist colony. Police are looking into it.

How do you make an elephant fly?
Well for a start you'll need a two-metre zip!

Y

YELLOW

> YELLOW AND GREEN ARE THE TWO MOST HILARIOUS COLOURS IN THE RAINBOW — CHECK GREEN JOKES ON PAGE 78

What's **yellow** on the inside and green on the outside?
A banana dressed up as a cucumber!

What's **yellow** and swings from cake to cake?
Tarzipan!

see more Jungle jokes on page 94

What's **yellow** and dangerous?
Shark infested custard!

★ Old ★ Chestnut Award

What else is **yellow** and dangerous?
A canary with a sub-machine gun.

What's **yellow** and writes?
A ball-point banana.

What's **yellow** and white and goes down railway tracks at a hundred miles an hour?
A train driver's egg sandwich.

YO-YO
Who invented the **yo-yo**?
Robert the Bruce after watching that spider!

NEWSFLASH:
A ship loaded with **yo-yoes** has hit a rock.
It sank fifty-two times.

YOUNG LADY
There was a **young lady** from Ryde
Who ate a green apple and died.
The apple fermented
Inside the lamented
And made cider inside 'er inside!

*★ Old ★
Chestnut
Award*

There was a **young lady** from Twickenham
Whose boots were too thick to walk quick in 'em.
After a mile
She sat down on a stile
And took off her boots and was sick in 'em!

There was a **young lady** from Riga
Who rode, with a smile, on a tiger!
They returned from the ride
With the lady inside,
And the smile on the face of the tiger!

COME ON, MAJOR, ONLY ONE
LETTER LEFT!

Z

ZEBRA

What do you call a **zebra** with no stripes?
A horse!

A **zebra** is just a horse in pyjamas.

What did the Wally call his **zebra**?
Spot!

What do you get if you cross a **zebra** with a pig?
Striped sausages!

What's black and white and goes round and round?
*A **zebra** in a revolving door!*

What's black and white and red all over?
*An embarrassed **zebra**!*

What do you get if you cross a **zebra** with a sheep?
A stripy sweater.

What do you get if you cross a **zebra** with a sheep and a kangaroo?
A stripy sweater with pockets.

ZOO

IS THE WRITING ON THE ZOO WALL CALLED GIRAFFITI?

NEWSFLASH:
Precious birds have been stolen from the **zoo**. The Flying Squad are looking into it.

ZZUB ZZUB

What goes **zzub zzub**?

A bee flying backwards!